DreamProjX:

A Guide to Creative Freedom and Economic

Independence for Designers, Inventors, and

Innovators

Table of Contents

The information and content contained in this Book is not intended to constitute legal advice, and you should contact an attorney before relying on any such information and content.

Author's Note

Because I am a designer, it feels natural to use the term "designer" fairly regularly throughout this book. What I mean by the word in this context, however, is something more all-encompassing than strictly those individuals within the design field. Whether they be engineers, inventors, scientists, artists, sculptors, or marketers, this book is for innovators of all kinds, and throughout the narrative I will be describing for them a specific way of doing business that has proven itself to me in the past.

From where I stand, there are three different benefits to be had here. The first is the business model itself, as an alternative way in which an innovator can realize creative and financial independence. Just as important for some readers however will be the chance to learn, through observing our company's experiences, that this model is not right for them—that they are better off saving themselves the time and financial investment that it would take to do what we have done. Whichever the case may be, the third and most important goal is in sharing the mindset that comes with this model, and how it can be used in realizing one's broader goals and dreams.

—

Preface:

No Secret Handshake

There seems to be a basic law of small talk that states that after that first brave "what is it that you do," most of us will say just about anything to keep the conversation moving along. Someone says that he's a dairy farmer, and suddenly you're telling him you have switched from two-percent to skim. You tell him you're a plumber, and he'll tell you all about last time that his drains got clogged.

When your profession is in the field of general product design, these conversations tend to take on a particularly confessional tone, as, one by one you find yourself being let in on hundreds of sheepish small disclosures about things that people wish they could invent. Slowly, after enough dinner parties and road-trips and long lines at Costco, you begin to become sensitive to the fact that innovation—at least, mentally-performed innovation— is not only done by people in the innovative line of work.

The legitimacy of the designs I hear about ranges as much as the individuals themselves. Sometimes the products really are "inventions" in the zaniest sense of the word, with everything but the coil springs and the cuckoo noises. Having said that, I am always surprised at how frequently I end up hearing some genuinely intriguing proposals—ideas that make me sit back midway through the conversation and think: this could really be something. This person's got something big. Some of the people I talk to are full-force in their ambition, ready to overhaul their whole careers in the hopes that a design deal could come through. Others want nothing more than simple patent rights before they hand it off. Almost always though, there's an all-American desire to *do* something with it, to not allow a scheme like that to die.

  Early on in my years as a professor, I realized that there was a certain nature-over-nurture element to design, a certain you-have-it-or-you-don't, and that everything else—connections, credentials, what-have-you—was supplementary to that. I could help most any student attain a certain degree of improvement in their work over the course of a term. But the great ones had always been great. From the first day they sat down at their desks, they had the eye of a designer and the thought patterns of a designer and the instinct of a designer built into their brains. Naturally, formal training is ideal. But the fact remains that it's possible to be brilliant without any schooling, in the same way that it's possible to have advanced degrees from the best design schools in the world and still be ridiculously bad at design.

There was a particular professor from design school whom I hold to be one of the most vital mentors of that time in my life. Apart from schooling us on the subject of design itself, he taught us to understand that we were not just students waiting for our turn to enter into the design world. We were, in fact, designers. And this concept—of "being," rather than "wanting to be," of not needing anyone's permission— is as true for my interns now as it was for me those forty years ago. The manuscript of *Moby Dick* was found in an old sea trunk and published when the man who wrote it was already in his grave. Should we then say that Herman Melville never was a writer? You don't need a product on the shelves of the local Wal-Mart or awards from long-named institutions or a resume listing all the best schools of design. There is no secret handshake, no password to get in. You are a designer simply by virtue of the fact that you design. And so apart from all the talk of business plans and financial freedoms that this book will cover, the underlying idea is that your work is worth something—that your work has value— and that you are right to want to share in your creations' financial success.

This is not a get-rich-quick book, nor is it an in-depth graduate-school-level tome on design or business—nor will I speak in reckless superlatives promising to provide you with "everything you need to know." What I can offer, however, are some carefully discerned thoughts about the opportunities and pitfalls of the field at hand. For the student at his drafting table at RISDE—the design consultant looking for the next step for his firm— the kid hunched over all the bottles of epoxy and Legos that his parents keep thinking he by now should have outgrown—this is what I've got to give.

—

Background—Robson Splane IDSA:, Pres. & CEO of Splane Design Associates, Inc., Founder of "DreamProjX" & Care-a-peutics., Co-founder of the fashion company Miriam J, Inc.

Born after WWII to a marine engineer and a former Disney animation artist, Robson Lindsay Splane Jr. was raised in the San Fernando Valley near Los Angeles during the last moments of the region's rural years. Aided by the advantage of being raised in an innovative family and a forward-thinking region, Splane's natural strong-points had him suited for the profession of industrial design long before he ever knew its name. He discovered it, however, during the course of his studies at Cal State Northridge, and went on to further his studies in the field both at Cal State Long Beach's prime design department and at Pasadena's distinguished Art Center College of Design, ultimately earning a B.A., two Master's Degrees and an M.F.A. (equivalent Ph.D.) over the course of his time at all three schools.

Having completed more than twice the amount of usual work required for students of industrial design, Splane went on to teach at two of his alma maters as well as at UCLA, ultimately tying up his formal education with a period of study overseas. Within a year of his return from Europe he married painter and designer Miriam Delarosa, who joined him in his design consulting firm in the San Fernando Valley, north of L.A.

In the years that followed, Splane would develop the idea that, intangible though it was, would become his most personally valued innovation. Started in 2002 and flourishing rapidly in the years since its foundation, the business model now known as "DreamProjX" is the end-result of Splane reworking the standard career opportunities of design (i.e. corporate design, design education, and consulting/"design-for-hire") into a new career option that concurrently utilized a whole range of often-unexplored options, such as licensing to manufacturers, self-manufacturing, e-commerce, and sale of design rights.

Today Splane draws on more than thirty years of experience working with a broad range of companies and technologies, as well as on the experiences gained from the innumerable products that he has been a major part of in the past. His work has been featured in numerous books, magazines, and museum exhibitions, and he has been voted in as a strategic advisor on a board of directors for a well-known manufacturing firm. Three of Splane's designs are being marketed on television at the moment of this publication, and many others are in development or negotiation.

—

What the Hell is an Industrial Designer Anyway?

To begin with, it isn't a designer of factories. As much as the phrase sounds like it must have something to do with assembly lines and large equipment, I should explain right now that that is its own entirely separate line of work.

"Industrial designer" is actually a relatively terrible label, since it gives no fair clue as to what the profession is about. This wouldn't be so bad if there were at least a short straightforward definition to follow it up with, but there isn't. In fact, if I could offer you a list of reasons why *not* to become an industrial designer, one of the top ones would be that you'll likely spend now until retirement having to figure out a way to explain just what it is you do.

There aren't many of us—only about 40,800 practicing in the United States at the present moment. But much of what you use in your day-to-day life was worked on by an industrial designer. Traditionally, we are the people that companies go to to develop the aesthetics and function of products that they have in mind. There's a whole range of specialties within the field. There are industrial designers who excel in electronics, and those who excel in transportation; there are some designers that companies go to for the designing of entire environments, and others that are best known for their children's toys. Our own company has worked on products from a fairly broad range of categories—everything from children's toys and automotive accessories to robotic medical equipment. On a whole, industrial designers can almost be described as being architects for things instead of buildings: everything that goes into creating that house on the corner, we do for any range of items that belong within it—or in the local hospital, or school, or gym, or on your person, or in your car.

As oxymoronic as it sounds, an industrial designer is someone who specializes in being a generalist, someone who is able to draw, sculpt, weld, blacksmith—program a computer-controlled machining station—operate a solid modeling computer. They need to be able to understand physics, mechanics, and electronics, as well as the ergonomics and anthropometrics that turn hard cold 'function-only' prototypes into comfortable appliances suitable to human needs. One might say that even a certain amount of psychology comes into the mix—certainly a degree of perceptiveness or at least a heightened common sense is necessary in this line of work when it comes to assessing hundreds of details and knowing what needs to be added (or what's trickier, eliminated) in order to bring in what's intuitive and get rid of what's unwieldy.

One of the biggest defining characteristics of design is that it demands an ability for not only a very practical understanding of things like pulleys and pinions but also a very artistic intuition. The best industrial designers are the ones who possess, or at least can muster, a certain dexterity with delicate details and a discernment for form and line and simply what looks "right." Generally in the world's workforce, there are the people who make things work right and there are the people who make things look right. Industrial designers are the overlap in the Venn diagram; they are the exception to the rule. The prototypical industrial designer is someone who lives in a world of table saws and engine lathes, who's got a grisly-looking chunk of keratin missing from his thumbnail from the last time he got his hand caught in a jig—but who, without so much as cracking a smile, could talk to you about color theory and texture more fluently than the most flamboyant wedding planner you have ever seen. Because as designers, we are responsible not only for the function of a product but for its marketability, its perceived value, its ease of use. It's all a part of what we do.

Traditionally, industrial designers fall into one of four basic categories. For the sake of discussion we'll call them types A, B, C, and D.

Type A are what they usually refer to as "corporate designers"—in-house designers working for a company, designing specifically what that company works on. If you are, for example, a corporate designer for a phone company, you work designing phones. Type B is consulting designers. A design consultancy is a team of designers that steps in for numerous businesses that may not have corporate designers of their own—they call on them as they need them, knowing that although they're not company employees they'll be able to get the job done. Type C consists of design manufacturers—designers who manufacture and market their own products—and Type D would be design educators—those who apply their design skills towards the aim of training other designers.

We started out as a Type B but over time evolved into something of our own, a "Type E," I suppose, a sort of a Type-B-turned-inside-out. Instead of having manufacturing companies come to us with products they had for us to work on, we began going to them with

20

products of our own initiative that we would still in part own once the deal was signed. Throughout this text, we will refer to this method simply as licensing.

Licensing—be it to industry or to infomercial companies—allows the product developer to create the product without having to be involved in manufacturing, sales, distribution, fulfillment, and customer service. It also gives the developer the ability to fully implement his or her creative abilities— as licensors we have the luxury of working with designs that had significance to us, rather than simply designing anything that we were asked to design. And so there was a definite emancipation in our decision to license rather than consult.

Over the years, however, licensing has become more and more of a difficult bartering process, particularly within the infomercial world. In recent years corporate attentions have brought growth to larger infomercial firms, causing small and even medium-sized ones to suffer for lack of funds. By our rationale, this leaves us with only the large corporations, who either don't accept licenses or who—when they do look outside their in-house design staff for ideas— offer minimum-percentage royalties, only to be had through fraught negotiations with gatekeepers and in-house legal councils.

And so in recent times, we as a company have actually begun to explore new directions, ways that lay beyond Types A, B, C, D, and even E. We will still be moving ahead with what licensing we can do; in fact, we have a licensing opportunity pending even during the writing of this. But whether or not we get a license has ceased to be a make-or-break situation for our products, and in as recently as the past year we have cut back dramatically on licensing in general and infomercial licensing in particular. Instead, we are turning our attentions towards selling our products on our own, with an eye towards options such as self-manufacturing and e-commerce. Because there *are* options, ones that can help designers to profit as much as licensing or more, and they're options on which we'll be expounding as we update this book over time.[1]

———

---

[1] For those reading this in its e-book form, know that anyone who has purchased the original edition will have rights to any future editions made within two years without additional cost.

Why Listen to a Designer?

The truth is that you do need to listen to attorneys
and MBAs. They can be an excellent source of advice on
everything from marketing to intellectual property to
patents and spreadsheets and everything in between. But if
you're searching for information regarding the creation of a
new product, or the financial autonomy that you might
realize from it, then maybe you should also be taking
something in from the people who are directly involved in
it.

Speaking personally—we enjoy what we do, but it
isn't a hobby; it's not something that we dabble in in our
off-time. It's what we've done professionally for decades
on hundreds of projects. They range from designs for
Sirius Satellite Radio in New York to furniture for Far East
America in Indonesia, from lighthearted projects for Walt
Disney and Universal Studios to more serious work for
Lockheed Aircraft and Teledyne Corporation. Through
our involvement on the Magic Bullet and our projects for
Sunkist, we've had a presence in the American household;
we've had a hand in cosmetology through Liz Claiborne
and Max Factor, and through our innovations for Pacific

Fitness and Thigh-Master we have helped keep people fit. When we weren't entertaining children with our Sega game controllers for Ascii International, we were helping to teach them through our products by Educational Insights. Most critically of late, we have taken people out of pain with the world's only robotic CPM device for the human spine. These projects and more are the real basis of our education, and the fodder for the insights that we'd like to share.

I don't have all the answers to the topics that would be addressed by business experts and lawyers, and so I'll gladly leave all that to those who are best at it. But I do think that for any new innovator looking for assistance in launching a product, a designer can offer a valuable perspective on mistakes to be avoided and benefits to be had.

A Selection of Splane's Designs

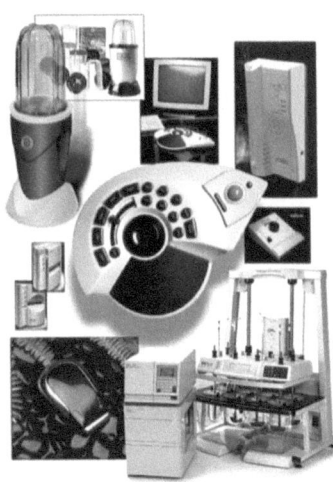

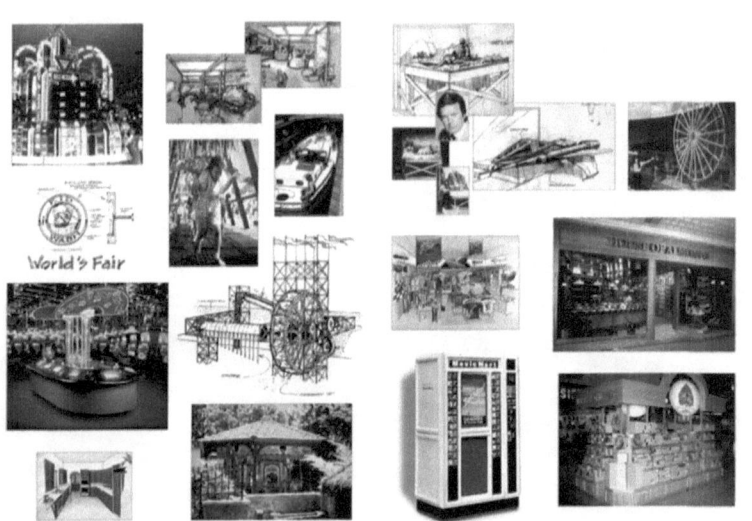

World's Fair

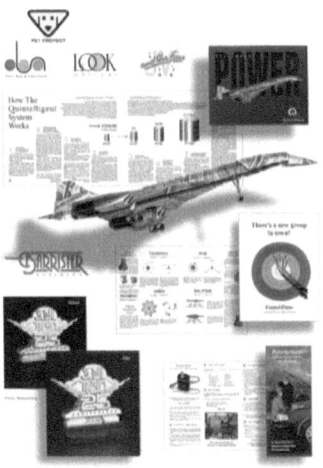

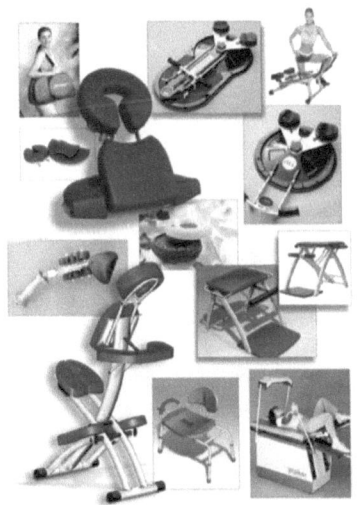

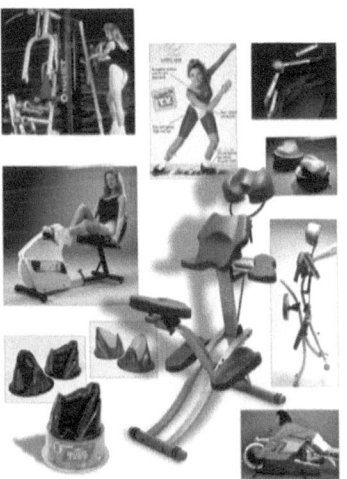

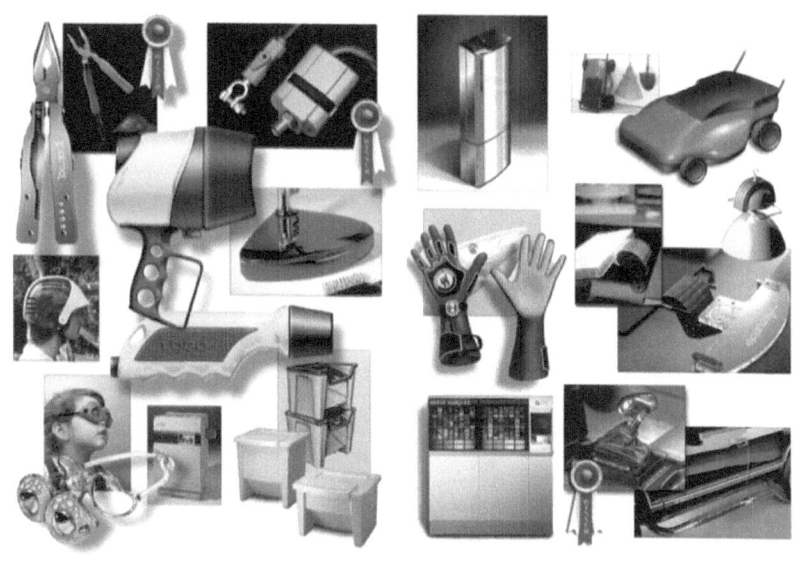

Our Story:

The Crapshoot

From Consultancy to Licensing Company

Splane Design Associates wasn't conceived with the aim of making a lot of money per se. From the moment that my twenty-four year old self started schemes on my own firm, the dream itself was simple: to create a small self-contained home-property studio, buzzing with the energy of a handful of sharp-eyed, quick-minded, creative-souled designers all working together to come out with truly fine work.

Not more than a few months after we were married, Miriam arrived home at our rented pad one day with the excited declaration that she'd found an old deserted clapboard house on a pine tree-lined street just around the corner from where we lived. Well, it wasn't the Pickfair Estate by any means. Stripped of plumbing and spray-painted Forest Service Green, the place was one half of an old California ranch house that (presumably at the hands of a particularly enterprising realtor) had very literally been cut in two. It was a piece of work, to be sure, but we were designers after all. Once the two of us stopped gaping we stepped back, squinted, cocked our heads a little, and then against all solid reason, cased the joint and decided to put down a bid. In a frenetic frenzy of primer, paint thinner, forklifts, and brick, the little green disaster started to take form as a place that could be lived in—and what's more, worked in. We weren't simply going about the work of turning a house into a home; we were creating a setting for a studio that could exist alongside it.

It was a wonderful sort of existence, those early years. The studio and shop that we built on the property became a place of intensity— of hard thinking, and mad focus, and all the energy of a handful of guys who were good at what they did throwing themselves into getting things done. But there was no avoiding certain splashes of just sheer spontaneous fun—my memories of the work we did are scenes of ravenous young interns crowded around the dinner table after we'd closed shop for the day, of afternoons where the children would be out there on stools at the wood lathes with shower-caps holding their hair back from their faces, of everyone racing into Miriam's kitchen to steal a gourmet spatula in the midst of a shop experiment, then coming back shaking with silent laughter as they held up the warped half-melted tool. Somehow, against all odds, the place became a world all its own.

The small studio: 1984-2003

Over the years however, the staff in the little studio occasionally climbed to as many as ten bodies sharing only about 1300 square feet; we were soon crowding extra drafting tables in amidst the machinery, and moving modeling out into the courtyard just to keep from trampling on each other's work. On top of this, the damage of the devastating Northridge earthquake of '94 and the growth of our young family meant that things were more than just a little cramped.

The guys in the studio were enthusiastic when we brought up the prospect of moving to a larger shop; the idea of a bigger work area with an upstairs conference room and an area dedicated to photography had them feeling full-steam ahead. As for myself—I'd spent years aiming for the next college degree, the next challenge, the next step forward, so to speak. I wasn't sure that it was in my nature to subscribe to the idea of bigger being better, but at that moment, going big just seemed like what to do. And so in the summer of 1994 we rolled up our sleeves, got out the crates and dollies, and leased offices in an industrial borough of Chatsworth, California, known at that time as the computer hard drive capital of the nation. (It actually turned out to be the pornography capital of the nation as well, as our neighbors next door at Forbidden Films could ascertain.)

The big studio: 1994-1998

Setting up the new studio was fun, but when it came to actually running it—well, that was something else again.

In our first year there, our gross sales went up 400%, our personal income went up only 10%, and my personal stress level was hiked higher than both figures combined. With so much new business coming in we soon had to re-open our original little studio as a second office just to keep up with the work, but during the lulls between jobs Miriam and I spent most of our savings just to keep our team employed. Not too long afterwards the Asian financial crisis hit, leaving us six figures into our credit lines and owing taxes on another half a dozen still. I rarely saw Miriam or our daughters, I'd become more of a salesman than a designer, and I found myself sinking deeper into a depression, longing for a simpler life than the one I led. It wasn't only that I wanted to go back to the way things were at the little office in the early days. Things by now had gone beyond that.

I'd grown up in that same valley long before it had become the maze of traffic and tract housing that it was. Every Seven-Eleven or seedy chain-linked parking lot that I passed each day I'd known once as a horse ranch, or as an orchard where kids used to pelt oranges at each other from behind the cover of old logs. That slow mid-century world was gone now; I'd watched it leave as I had come into my prime, and I'd thought that I had learned to live without it in my life. But somehow now, I found myself wanting to return to it, or to something like it. Miriam met the idea of rural life gamely; as the daughter of one of the governors of Micronesia she'd lived her little girlhood on remote islands all over the Pacific, and had more no attachment than I did to suburban sprawl. But it was a castle in the air nonetheless, and as beautiful as the vision was to us I couldn't realistically envision anybody hiring a designer who was located in a barn at the end of some bumpy dirt road, no matter how charming the pastoral view might be.

There had been a time some years earlier when I'd started thinking about alternative ways of running a company. We had been to several meetings with various clients who had mentioned certain small frustrations in passing—"Argh, if we could just find someone who would design a product that could solve such-and-such, we would make a fortune..." they used to say. Driving home from these meetings, our designers always ended up scratching their heads. Well hell, we shrugged; why didn't they just do it themselves? It wouldn't be much of a big deal...

Well, naturally it wasn't a big deal from our standpoint—it was what we did. There were things within our ability, however, that did not come naturally to everybody else. And as we realized this, the first thought for a new business model was born: hypothetically, we could take on whatever project that they wanted, not charging them a dime in terms of flat-out hiring fees, but asking for a license and royalties. It was a great beginning. But ultimately we hit an ethical block. Suppose that after their having given us their ideas, and after our having done the work and given them first right of refusal and so forth—they weren't able to go through with it? Legally, there was nothing preventing us from offering it to someone else. That said, doing so didn't seem to us to be a very decent or fair-minded kind of action, and we knew it wasn't one we could allow ourselves to take.

It was a great disappointment to realize that the plan as a whole couldn't be taken any further. It had been a nice idea, and maybe an understandable one too… Things like that have a way of drifting through your mind from time to time after watching how much profit you are helping other people make and knowing that not much of it will come your way. But we couldn't resent the clients for their position; it was only right that the people who took the risks reaped the reward—and anyhow, we'd never been particularly ambitious where money was involved. The idea had always been to just make enough to be comfortable and have a nice little life, nothing more. And so, back during this time, we had turned out the proverbial lights and rolled down the proverbial warehouse doors on this new way of doing business, and for several years we simply let it be.

But by now, as I sat at my desk in the big empty Chatsworth office in the wee hours of the morning, staring into the wall, I knew that something had to change. It had been all right for a while, living hand-to-mouth month-by-month, but Miriam and I were trying to raise a family after having gone through our retirement savings twice in our attempts to keep our people employed, and there are moments in people's lives when they simply get worn down. It was time to start from scratch. If we were going to make the move to the country, this was the moment to do it; if we were going to switch our business model, now was the time. Somehow, the two seemed to go hand in hand, as I realized that only through changing the way that we did business would it be possible to ever make the move. We would redesign the old business model into a new one—"Dreamprojects," we called it—make it so that the products we were licensing were our own ideas from the very start, no messing around with other people's innovations. We'd be a smaller company but a better one—and for once, one with the power to sit down at a table with our clients as equals, making products that meant something to us and not needing the approval of anybody in the world.

The Valley Center shop and studio (here under
construction)
2004 – present day

—

"The Ranch" was what we had always called it, but really it was more than just a place. It was the ability to spend time with my family at the drop of a hat, to travel if I wanted to, to pursue projects of my own if they should arise. This hadn't been a realistic vision when we were working as a consultancy and being paid by the hour. Our profits were limited to how many designers we had and how many hours we worked in a day, and in order to make any substantial profits we had to have such a high employee headcount that it was impossible for me to work personally on my designs.

With the royalty system that came with licensing, however, it was possible for us to be earning profits even while we slept, and to actually be doing so for years on end. (In our licensing agreements there has never been any limit on the number of years for which we receive royalties. As long as the licensee[2] is making money, so do we.) It was like being a novelist whose books would keep making money long after they hit the shelves. Our original concept was to take a sort of a scattergun approach—if we licensed several products every year, and if even just one of each

---

[2] Also, a little bit of a cursory glance over the semantics involved in all of this: If you're the inventor, you're the licensor. If you're the company taking the product, you're the licensee. I'm sure you know this already, but they're easy to mix up if you're reading quickly, and for obvious reasons it's pretty important to keep the two distinct. As for the document itself, I might go back and forth between referring to it as a contract or an agreement or a license; just know that they're all simply different names for the same thing. I think I end up favoring 'license' the most in my writing and speech, probably out of some subconscious effort to sound as unthreatening as can be. I'm not sure how effective that is, but there you have it: there's a salesman in all of us, I guess.

year's products brought in some returns, then in ten years we'd be getting ten checks every quarter, the logic seemed to say. In practice, only on occasion did we have big hits, but when the hits did come they were so much bigger and more successful than all the small ones that in the end it did pay off. On a licensing/royalty-based system, we made more by having one hit every five years than we would have made by being paid by the hour for five years straight.

I've never dreamt of retirement—even now, in my sixties, there are mornings when I think it might be nice to work until I die. But I want to know that I don't *have* to work until I die. Licensing was my first large-scale attempt to secure that for myself.

From Licensing to Self-Manufacturing

And it worked, to an extent.

Licensing was what gave us a new lease on life—it let us get out of the restraints imposed by design-for-hire, and has been serving us well for years. Some of our best successes have arrived through licensing, and so we have a special history with it. But the licensing process itself— the business politics and bartered percentages, the courting of prospective licensees for every new design— it can be tense work. It isn't work we mind, because the ultimate liberation does so much to make up for it. But after years of licensing, the question eventually presented itself: was there a way to create our own ideas and realize profits while avoiding the more difficult elements that the licensing process held? We struggled with these questions for years, and ultimately, self-manufacturing was the answer that turned up.

There are certain challenges involved in traditional self-manufacturing (essentially, erecting one's own smoke stacks). It's a large investment with long lead times, little flexibility, and little time for innovation. It also involves the question of whether or not you want to have to deal directly with badly-machined parts or with Frank from the assembly line who never showed up for work.

For these reasons, we have decided to turn our focus to a form of self-manufacturing that allows us to instead hire out the individual manufacturing chores (molding, stamping, etc.) and results in our selling through wholesale, retail, or e-commerce.[3] Through this system, services are

---

[3] Any one of which might (ironically) even lead you back to licensing— in the instance of the product becoming successful through these various non-licensing means, a designer might very well find him- or herself being courted by interested licensees somewhere later down the line.

outsourced to companies that act as factories on our behalf, so that everything from the packaging and shipping to the accounting is in their hands.[4]

By doing this, we are not abandoning licensing altogether. We are, however, creating a strong supplementation for it.

This expansion of our business model has already led to an increase in our options and abilities as a company. Drawing from the forty-plus products ready-and-waiting in our proverbial back rooms, we've begun to look into grouping together similar innovations and building small firms around each group, which we would then operate using a mixture of licensing, e-commerce, product rights sales, and (most strongly) self-marketing.

We might have Rehab and Fitness in one company, "green" products in another, independent living products in a third—we might even form companies around a single product. Some of the products would be innovations close to our hearts. Others would simply serve to fund other innovations. Whatever our level of personal attachment to them, the withstanding idea would be to implement

---

[4] There still are drawbacks, however, not least of which is that you may need to be up for multiple trips to China, and will likely be promised "no problem, no problem" in situations where there may be a very big problem indeed.

products that, although they might not be trendy in an as-seen-on-TV type of a way, are timeless and solid and do not lose demand.

The purpose for there being several different companies rather than one large manufacturing firm is twofold. For one thing, it simply makes things more manageable to have everything divided up by the nature of the design. For another, it isolates the liability of the firms; should any of the firms be sued, it acts as a precaution against any domino effect falling into place. The fact that we'd have three or four companies would not necessarily mean we'd have to have three or four of everything where infrastructure is concerned. Each firm would be in possession of its own manager or president and might each have its own C.E.O., but eventually, there might be an umbrella company that would double as a holding company for the I.P., protecting our patents and reducing multiplication of effort within the companies that it controls.

In executing this multi-company endeavor, we realize we may have to go against our natural instinct and account for the need for investors. It isn't enough to have a dazzling array of innovations; a firm has to be "safe." There's got to be a bankable team of managers hitting home runs, a real business plan that's something more than just an outline or a map. In many cases there's going to need to be an exit strategy as well, since investors are at some point going to wish to cash-out by selling the company and receiving a lump sum.

And so we're only in the infancy of this. We still need the marketing people and the C.E.O.s and the accountants—there's a good deal that goes into this sort of a thing. But I think there's something to be said for companies like Hewlett Packard in its early years, or like Steve Jobs' Apple—I think there is a place for companies that are directed by the innovators themselves, without doing things strictly by a cost analysis.

I don't think I'm alone in this opinion. There's been a growing trend of innovators as entrepreneurs; it seems to be less and less uncommon to hear of creatives rejecting the consultancy path for newer production methods and greater rewards.

This is our particular version of that. This is our next step towards taking power back.

Complementary Skill Sets

If it sounds as if this growth is a departure from the spirit of our company—if it seems as if we've gone from big to small only to fall into going big again—then I should take a moment to clarify.

At almost exactly the same time that we decided to move forward with the creation of spin-off companies, we began to newly recognize the necessity of partnering with business specialists, negotiators, distributers, investors, and angels, who would leave us to focus our attentions on design.

Working with complementary skill sets is not just a matter of our only wanting to do the "fun part." It's a matter of efficiency. I think most designers would agree with the idea that by and large, it's rare to find strong business-sense and strong creativity within the same individual. Some of the major innovation schools have recently begun programs that bring in mentors who have contacts to venture capitalists, with the aim of teaching design students to be MBAs. It's always a heartening thing to see schools make efforts to help their students become more well-rounded. Without wanting to sound too pessimistic, however, I have a feeling that expecting a designer to write a brilliant business plan is just as unrealistic as trying to teach a CEO to design and engineer a complicated product.

Regardless of whether or not designers *can* "do it all," I believe it's unnecessary—and even counterproductive—for them to try to. If an innovator has someone else running his or her business, he or she is able to systematically move from creating one product to creating the next. However, if that same innovator has to act as his or her own business manager, then managing spreadsheets, business plans, funding, permits, and certificates will most likely make for a certain amount of creative inefficiency.

In theory, I'd like to be able to design a product, hand it over to a partner and their team, and have them take it through the full manufacturing and sales process while I go back to doing what I do best. I'd like to have my own crew of designers remain small and nimble, but have my partner's staff grow as large as it needs to be.

With this in mind, I began looking for a deal that was fair both to my prospective business partner and to myself. I was not able to offer an exorbitant salary, but it seemed to me that any partner who signed with me had rights to a comfortable percentage of our declared profits, or, vested over several years, a certain amount of stock or back-end ownership of the company, so that if and when we did sell the company he or she had a certain percentage of that sale. It was important to me also that I as the innovator did not end up working for the partner, as happens so much of the time, and that compensation was performance-based— that we'd be working with someone who was willing to put, as they say, "a little skin in the game." I was seeking an individual who shared with me a common set of beliefs about what was fair and what wasn't— but who, when it comes to weaknesses and strengths, was not another "me."

We interviewed extensively and spoke with a high number of interested individuals, but much of the time it seemed we came away with the concern that they held a disproportionate focus on their own immediate fiscal welfare, rather than in what they could bring to the company.

Some time ago, however, we had the excellent fortune of being introduced to Greg Szabo, whose talents and character we soon came to regard very highly, and with whom we have been working ever since.

Mr. Szabo is a seasoned executive of 35+ years who has Sales, Marketing and General Management experience with both public and private companies, including Becton

Dickinson, Zimmer, Sunrise Medical and MultiCell Technologies. Most recently, he was the Interim COO at an Orange County based electronics recycling firm. He received his Bachelor's Degree from the University of Toledo and his Master's Degree in Management from the Peter Drucker School of Management at Claremont University.

Additionally, we have joined forces with Al Diem, who has worked in the Direct to Consumer industry for the past fifteen years, and who for the past seven years has been specifically focused on marketing and ROI based TV and Digital Advertising. Mr. Diem has managed campaigns that have sold cumulatively over 30 million units in combined direct to consumer and retail focused campaigns, and is an expert at using technology to strategically maximize ROI. He helped launch, and currently consults for, a Direct to Consumer Digital Advertising company; most recently, he was the Director of Marketing for Hampton Direct, at the time a leader in short form Direct to Consumer [Infomercial] Marketing.

Initially, he was expected to become a full time member of the Team; as new opportunities have come up for him, however, it has been agreed that he will continue on as a consultant.

In the past it's been tempting for us to want to oversee everything personally, to trust our own half-blindness more than someone else's clear vision. We've begun to realize what a mistake that is. We need individuals who love the tasks that to us are confusing, who excel at the things that we go out of our way to avoid. We've come to value them now more than ever before.

—

Why Now Is a Great Time to be an Innovator

When we first decided to leave consulting, a number of factors had fallen into place that made it a good time to make the move.

A lot of it had to do with alterations in patent law. Several years previously, the patent offices in the United States had developed what is now known as a provisional patent, and so for the first time, for the cost of $125, we could send to the patent office some very brief forms, drawings, specifications and renderings, and thereby establish legal patent pending for one year. We no longer had to negotiate with nothing but a non-disclosure agreement to protect us throughout all the time it took for a full-fledged multi-thousand dollar patent to come through. The provisional patent had arrived, and it turned out to be a savior of sorts.[5]

Obviously too, there were changes in technology. It probably seems like a matter of course to anyone entering the workforce at the present moment, but I think even those readers must have some perception of how big a difference

---

[5] Provisional patent form: http://www.uspto.gov/forms/sb0016.pdf

it was (or "must have been") to go from typewriters and white-out to high-tech computers, or what a shock it was to change from booking business flights across the world to showing our work across the world without even standing up from our desks. With the emergence of Power Point and similar presentation programs, we could put together an entire pre-production display. Where patents were concerned, just by typing into a Google search-box we were able to quickly and efficiently scope out what was already out in existence through the use of a preliminary search, rather than going straight to a patent attorney and potentially paying thousands of dollars to have it sniffed out.

Technology has come to play a strong role for our communication and presentation, but it's done more than that; it's had a direct role in the craft itself as well. The fact that we are able to create almost photo-realistic images of still-unrealized products is something that is incredibly useful to us in communicating our vision to and amongst ourselves. I do still believe in designers learning to draft by hand; in my opinion, the new technology is something that should only be a tool, a complement to the old skills more than a substitution of them. There is something almost sad in the idea that fundamental hand skills are being lost. But the truth is, nearly all of our rendering in recent years has been through computer rendering—in fact, such is the technology of the moment that even some of our three-dimensional shop models can now be created by digitally programming certain information and having them spit out, layer-by-layer, by computer-linked machines.

Sometimes, the changes have not been quite so obviously positive, and it has required a bit of perspective to see them as opportunities rather than the massive fiascos they initially appear to be. When economic circumstances first started creating sizable cutbacks on research and development, we were informed by various experts that it was going to be necessary to make some drastic compromises in the way we did our licensing agreements. With respect to our advisors, we disagreed and still do. To us it seemed very clearly an opportunity: without new products, these manufacturing and marketing companies would become stagnant and would suffer. They would die. The fact that we were able to offer them products which they had put no money into developing elevated us into a position of far greater equality when sitting down for negotiations.

I think that as Americans of the twenty-first century, we're all very used to the idea that our country is going through a difficult period. We hear it all the time, and we say it all the time, and we hear it and we say it because it's true. But what doesn't get said or heard is that there are a few small fields within this very same economy that have never known a moment as golden as right now. To be an innovator in the United States at this point in the new millennium—you're starting off with more advantages than were had by any of the innovators in the generations leading up to now. And what innovators they were! Americans, I think, are innovative almost to the point of it being a cultural tradition. I'm not quite sure what it is that makes this nation such a hotbed for crazy new inventions and ideas and fads—maybe it's in the gene pool, after generations of wild courageous thinkers drawing here from all across the globe. Whatever the reason, this is a place where bold thinking thrives. The United States doesn't have a prayer when it comes to competing with Asia in cost-effective manufacturing, and a good many countries besides the U.S. have high technologies and their own talented designers and engineers. But because of our instinct towards innovation, we in this country have never lost the opportunity to compete.

—

A Word on Working for Oneself

There's a whole messy slew of reasons why starting up a company of one's own is not for everyone, and I should be upfront about that. Once you begin, you'll find there is no regular paycheck, no health coverage, no sick leave or paid vacation. Even if someone has the willingness to face these disadvantages, they might not have the natural disposition it requires. There's a certain amount of self-governance that goes into setting the hours you follow to the hilt even when there's no one there see, to block out the distractions of family and friends who don't recognize your work as Work... There are plenty of people who would love to work for themselves but who know that if they tried it, they would be in their pajamas every day till noon. And that's completely understandable; it's natural to need outside pressure in order to be able to work. It's just that it's important to be sure to make your career decision is in accordance with that fact.

Apart from the discipline aspect, there are matters of risk to take into account. Many of the independent types of design work that we discuss here *do* end up being very lucrative, but that is only if they pass all the hurdles. With licensing, for example—to begin with, can you find someone to whom you can present your ideas? Do they sign on the bottom line? If they sign, do they include you in their insurance policy the way they should? Do they ever actually send you your advance; if they do, do they have funding? (Because if they can't afford fairly nominal investments, which you will repay from royalties, you've got to wonder how they're going to afford tooling or inventory or TV time...) Let's say they do have funding. Will they agree to indemnify you—that is to say, if there should be a lawsuit that involves the product, are they sure to have your back? Do they roll the product out on schedule, assuming that they follow through with tooling and production? If the product sells do they send you your royalty, for every bit that you are due?

Even once all of this is said and done, it's easily a year before anything gets out on the market; we've had products that have been waiting in the wings for a decade or more. And that's not to mention the simple question of "is the product a success?" The truth of the matter is that there are only a relatively small number of hits each year, and even if all these things go well and the project's a success, you have to take into account whether or not the product will get counterfeited or knocked off by someone else. As long as there are good products in the world, there will be people thinking that the profits in some way should be theirs.

We've worked with people who have left their day jobs too soon, and who have realized (with equal promptness) that that decision was something they could not afford. There are very few over-night triumphs in the innovation world. Design is a risky business in the most unglamorous sense of the term, and one whose rewards are slow to come; you have to do whatever it takes to keep the lights on until your successes give you the freedom to quit.

This book is largely targeted at individuals who are interested in a less conventional form of business and living, but before we even get too far into that, it's important for readers to be able to discern from the onset whether or not that is who they are. We've made millions of dollars doing this, but we've also spent millions in learning what we've learned. There's nothing wrong with wanting something steadier, something that is simply good solid work that can be counted on. The majority of people out there would be on some level opposed to leaving themselves vulnerable in the way that DreamProjX requires, and it's got nothing to do with talent. Not everybody is going to succeed at the DreamProjX model: take what works for you and leave the rest.

—

Sailing to Tahiti

Somewhere during the early 1970s, when I was just into my twenties and still discovering design, I found myself working my way through school as a deckhand aboard old wooden sailing vessels chartering between the West Coast and the Caribbean.

Throughout my seven years of seamanship I learned that there is a certain unspoken culture among seamen that isn't written about in any manual of rigging or knots. Some of it has do with a certain disgust for laziness, and an instinct for dependability, an ability for humor under fear or stress. A good deal of it also has to do with thinking ahead.

The islands we chartered to were just a small series of dots in the Caribbean Sea, but I knew that so long as we had our compasses and chart, we had a fair chance of reaching our terminus. Had we shoved off empty-handed, with just a vague optimism that we would randomly bump into our destination in 139 million square miles of open sea...I won't insult your common sense by telling you how slim the odds would be.

It was some years into my career as a designer before I realized that plotting charts is not for nautical men alone. All of us are out there sailing, when it comes to futures being formed. Some are as sharp as Admiral Nelson at the helm; others are drooling in their bunks below decks, occasionally poking their heads out to get a glimpse of how the sea gulls look that day. The first type doesn't require anything to be said to them; the second type is beyond doing anything about.

But there is a third category to be accounted for— the ones that are out there steering madly without a single thought of looking at the charts. Usually, there are no charts—they never drew them up. They may know with a passion where they want to lay their anchor, but nothing more than that.

It's completely normal to be intimidated at the onset, but eventually we have to get serious about this business if we're going to begin to talk about doing it at all. A plan is imperative—moreover, a detailed plan is imperative. Start big. Look at where you are and where you hope to end up. Plot out all the major stops and turning points along the way. Then, zooming in, fill in the smallest details of the track. Working off of long term lists, year-long lists, daily lists—putting onto paper big goals as well as incremental ones and setting deadlines for yourself—you will find that bit by bit, things will have a way of getting done.

Some of my biggest plans in business have worked out very differently from how I envisioned them. DreamProjX itself, in fact, was never my direct objective starting out. But had I not had any plan at all, I would have never even found the detours—detours which, funnily enough, often ended up being more of an oasis for me than what I originally thought I wanted as my destination.

—

Seafaring days in the West Indies—circa 1973-1980

Inspiration

It's got a reputation for being a bit of a stupid question, this issue of where-do-innovators'-ideas-come-from, and admittedly it *is* something of a circular inquiry in a way. To a certain degree, inspiration comes simply by the nature of What We Do. Designers *are* designers usually because they are idea people, and, when confronted with the question of how they come up with such ideas, will for once in their lives have absolutely no idea at all. That said, I think it's a bit pretentious for us to act as though it isn't a very natural thing to ponder, and so I'll take the liberty of asking the question for you, and will do my best to give a good response.

One very simple source of inspiration I can attest to is the practice of keeping a sketchbook. Sketchbooks have a way of being intimidating to some people—all those waiting and judgmental blank faces of pages. But you don't have to be able to draw like Leonardo; you don't even have to draw at all. There are no rules to what goes into a sketchbook. It could be magazine clippings, it could be charts, written abstracts of possible products—whatever gives you pause for thought. My own sketchbooks aren't anything particularly remarkable looking; they're just thick-paged, cardboard-covered spiral notebooks from the local art-supply, clamped shut with a binder clip and self-labeled with the year of use. I buy them to match as I go through them, and file each one away when it's ready to be retired, so that over the years I've built up whole shelves of a collection, decades' worth of thoughts. Often I don't think to revisit them—but they're there, and if I should come to a snarl on some current project, I know that I can stop and think, 'I'm pretty sure I had an idea once that would relate to this," and pull up something from thirty years ago that was useless at the time but just right for the here and now.

Beyond this, however, a great majority of inspiration simply comes down to one rather tired mid-Victorian cliché. Necessity is very much the mother of Invention, just as the embroidery samplers always pontificated from the wall. It happens almost automatically, the way that our thoughts are routinely spun from personal experiences and needs. It's a matter of noticing which small troubles we consistently up against, which sorts of products we keep wishing we could buy. Everyone has got those personal mundane irks that they run into day to day, and even if you should be weirdly fortunate enough to not have any, there will always be those who are more than willing to volunteer their own. Listening to the individuals around you and being attuned to what they want, "keeping your ear to the ground" so to speak—it all sounds just too easy, but don't overthink it. This is how it works.[6] One fellow I know of made a fortune by very simply going up to nurses at hospitals and asking them what they wished they had; once told, he'd promptly turn around and bring the products to life. Newspapers and periodicals are useful; I'm not much of a trend-minded man but in this line of work it *is* important to stay up to date with what kinds of changes are happening in the world. Sometimes there are gold mines to be had even in patent searches —seeing all that prior art can be discouraging, but it can get the ball rolling and have you thinking of everything that hasn't yet been done.

So think, and listen, and mostly be aware. This is the good part of design.

—

---

[6] If we do find someone who has a great inspiration, we believe it is important to remember to fold them into the mix where financial returns are concerned. Even if their involvement does not go any further than that one initial inkling, it's what got us going and we owe a lot to them, and it's necessary that they be taken care of and realize something for their thought,.

Getting Started

A strange thing happens when someone in the studio brings up an idea for a project.

The lunch table goes into a casual lull. Eyes lose focus just a bit; jaws shift, and heads nod a fraction here and there. I like it, someone throws out. No, I really think we should look into that, it's... it's Good. Ideas start to bounce around: What if you made it adjustable right at the base, then had a little lever that snapped up... or you could have it where it plugs into your car charger too...

And for one blessed moment, the creation is indulged with all the cautious reverence usually reserved for the sides of bassinets.

Then the next time that everybody meets, without missing a beat they take this beautiful wec bundle of innovative joy, give it a lightly anticipatory toss, then proceed to take turns hurling it against the wall to see if it will break.[7] Are there lawsuit liabilities? Prior patents? Sony's got something really similar—here, I picked one up this morning for us to fiddle around with, check it out.

---

[7] I realize this has rapidly morphed into what's either a remarkably mixed metaphor or a remarkably sick one, but we're going to press on.

And it goes on.

Here in the studio, we've got a long-established methodology of hurdles that the guys use to test a product after its inception: we'll try to save it where we can, we'll make adjustments on it if it lends itself to adjustments being made, but ultimately if it hits too many problems that it cannot clear, it gets killed—even if we like it a lot. I won't say that it's always painless; there are moments now and then when we're a bit like 4H kids giving up their favorite pig. But there's no sense spending time and funding in engineering it, doing prototypes, doing packaging and all the rest of it when the very nature of the product may be flawed. We can't afford to fall in love with everything we do, not when we'll probably have to mothball nine out of ten concepts right at hand.

So with this in mind, we plunge into the act of patent-searching. The early stages of this can usually be done on our own—since the arrival of the internet, the process has become much easier than it used to be. Both the U.S. Patent and Trademark Office (www.uspto.com) and Google Patents (www.googlepatents.com) have websites where anyone can type in a keyword and search for what is known as "prior art"—i.e. anything similar enough to your design that it might jeopardize its legitimacy.

While we're wading through our search results though, we have to keep in mind that not all the competition will be found on the patent lists. There *are* things just floating around out there patentlessly[8], and even though that's probably not the wisest way for their creators to be doing things, they're still not entirely unprotected. Patented or not, once a product is out on the market, the idea for it can't be patented by anyone else.[9]

If we don't come across anything worth worrying about in the files or on the shelves, it doesn't mean we're out of the dark—it simply means we want to hire a patent agent or patent attorney (also known as an intellectual property/"I.P." attorney) to do a real search with a fine-toothed comb. In the case that nothing comes up in the attorney's official search, we then go for a provisional patent, which is very simple and can be done ourselves, costing a little over a hundred dollars and lasting for a year.

---

[8] I'd like to take this moment to remind Microsoft Word and its sanctimonious red squiggles that William Shakespeare introduced over 1700 new words into the English language, every one of which is far more outrageous than adding two perfectly logical suffixes onto the word "patent."

[9] In instances like these, sometimes just purchasing a sample of what you're up against is the easiest way to investigate whether or not you'd be stepping on any toes.

Although it isn't necessary to have a provisional patent before obtaining an 'actual' one, a provisional can be rolled into the final patent application if and when you do decide to get one later down the line. It's an easy and affordable beginning, considering a full-fledged patent's cost. Around this time—or even before it—there is the composing of the "written concept." In the same way that a writer has to have a succinct summary of his or her novel to present to his editors before they look more deeply into taking the manuscript, a designer needs a single page abstract filled with bullet-points of why there is a need for what he or she is creating, how its solution is different from the rest, what the product's benefits are, and whether there's a market for it. In essence, you are putting all of the product's most important points into eight-and-a-half-by-eleven tangibility for somebody to read.

It's also right about now that we begin a collection of the product's documentation. From the very start, each product is given a thick three-ring binder that includes competition research, relevant patent info, concept sketches and engineering drawings, information on sourcing venders for making parts, correspondence records—it even has compartments for storing material swatches and business cards. In addition to this binder, every product gets a "tote," a simple box into which go all of the little physical things that relate to the product, be they samples we have bought, parts we have made, or small molds or jigs or experiments that are specific to the prototype's construction.

After written concepts and patent searches have been taken care of and proper documentation has begun, market research begins to come into the mix. Again this is an instance where the internet is a fantastic tool. We need to gauge the demographics of our likely purchasers, as well as to figure out their sheer quantity and how many of our products they are likely to consume over the course of a year. Competition research is essential too—what exactly is the pricing on the products that we are up against, and at whom exactly are they aimed? This is also the time that we'll begin thinking about what type of licensing or self-manufacturing or e-commerce we might want to use, and when we'll start making the connections that we need.

Meanwhile— we break out the clay.

This is the moment for design markers and tracing paper, for band-saws and jig-saws and foam-core forms— for all the rough little sketches and models that being a designer is all about, while we gradually carry our product from smoke-rings into solid form. If the product still is going strong after everything we've put it through by now, it is imperative to create a prototype, or a "breadboard," as they're occasionally called. We fiddle with it, we play with it and get a feel for it—maybe we make four or five or six different versions. It's fantastic if our working models resemble what we hope the finished product is going to be, but they don't have to. Right now, the goal is just to prove it works. Sometimes our early models actually do come out like they're supposed to; more often they look like something Rube Goldberg might have collaborated on with a Dada artist and a slightly insane child. Thankfully, our graphic designer is there with polished images of the final design to help the imaginations of the licensees as they gingerly prod at all the squeaking spinning plywood parts.

Design, when it comes right down to it, is an all-or-nothing kind of game, so if in your most honest moments you know that what you're doing isn't something feasible, you're better not to even start it—and when you do do it, you've got to be prepared to take it all the way. It isn't that you want to plug away futilely for years at something that is obviously not going to come to fruition, all for the sake of diligence. There is a balance, and your discernment will be key. But there is something to be said for sticking it out. People get to thinking that once they've got a prototype, they've got it made. The fact is, 40% of the sweat lies in the last 10% of the project, and even when you're 99% done there still are zero dollars in your hand. But as long as you're still working on that last percentage of completion, your product's not a flop. I always used to think that if I somehow made it in this industry, it would be creative skill that got me through. It turned out that endurance was every bit as big a deal.

—

Brainstorming:

Ideation and Conceptualization

Before you ever begin to schedule meetings regarding production, there is the meeting within your own team of developers that is known just as "The Brainstorm." It's what everything else centers around, and it deserves a chapter all its own.

Even if you aren't aware of it, you've seen what an innovative brainstorm looks like hundreds of times. Every time a new high-tech product comes out on the market, images of brainstorms are run all over the air—clusters of designers all hunched informally around a table, sketching intently with mechanical pencils and passing leaves of tracing paper for their colleagues to review—usually there are one or two shots of people tracing beautiful lines rather slowly on a white-board, and a couple of young men with crisp rolled sleeves and glasses talking with their hands about some idea that's rendered soundless by the montage music's smooth deep tones. It's the sort of thing that looks like it's just dreamed up for dramatic purposes. But apart from a bit of stagey flare and the fact that we're not half as well-dressed as these guys, this is one of the few cases where the theatrical representations in the ads are in fact not far from how it's done. This is where it all begins; this is what we do.

Time Magazine ran an article some time ago claiming that the benefits of brainstorming were an urban myth, that it was in short an ineffectual tool. I think Time's great. It spends a remarkable amount of time being trafficked and held ransom within the otherwise pacifistic home in which I live. But I have to say from personal experience that this article just can't be right. For one thing, basic math says that if you've got four designers in a brainstorm, you'll get four times your output. In fact, it comes out as even more than that. When we're talking about a setting where you've got individuals working off of one another, building off each other's best ideas and misinterpreting their worst ones into something altogether new… it's not so much four-times as four-squared.

It's always kind of nice to have those rare brainstorms that are just sort of off-the-cuff— the late-night end-of-the-New-Years-party gatherings where everybody, giving up the pretense of not thinking about design in their off-time, ends up huddled around the coffee table kicking around a new idea, sketching onto wine-stained cocktail napkins. As a rule however, the best discussions tend to have a certain amount of preparation behind them, and there's a lot of individual groundwork that goes into getting to where you're all ready to talk. By the time you sit down at the conference table on the morning of the brainstorm, you'll each have put hours into getting ready individually— poring over design books and magazines, researching different mechanisms and components, learning as much as possible about your product's field. Nowadays, the internet will most likely be the main resource; certainly it is the quickest way of starting to get answers to all the questions that must be asked. What's out there in the way of competition? Is your own product an improvement on it...more cost effective, at least? What companies might be interested in what you're doing—do they review outside ideas? Which brokers could help you connect with them? Or, another important thought to hold in mind at this point—what specific market are you designing for? When we were doing a filter heater for swimming pools a while back, we automatically assumed we'd be designing for the homeowner. Not so. It was the pool contractor. We found out what percentage of the time he was making the decision, what aspects of the product he took into account when making that decision (in this case, ease of installation), and generally researched to the point where we knew everything that could possibly be known about the average American pool man and could construct a corresponding product that would suit his wants and needs.

The brainstorm doesn't have to be a big gathering. In fact, it's best to keep it small. Having somewhere around four individuals present seems about right; I think if the headcount got any higher than eight my best judgment would be to break the group into two small sets. But however you arrange it, everyone who's there has got a role that they are filling.

First off, there's the chairman, or 'facilitator' if you will, who's got to be up there writing on the board and keeping track of time and generally managing the flow of things, prompting other members of the group. You'll want to have a couple of mechanically-inclined people who've got a solid sensibility about how a good product should interface with the people putting it to use; these are the designer-types, essentially. But of no lesser value (though lucklessly at risk of being overlooked) is the presence of specialists who are not necessarily schooled in design but who carry a significant understanding of the very specific market that is being approached. There was a product that had us researching diabetes a couple of years back, and we realized before sitting down for discussion on it that we were lucky enough to know someone who was (get this) not only a doctor but a diabetic one. We roped him into a brainstorm faster than you could prick your finger; I doubt the man had ever met any group of individuals so enthusiastic over his disease.

There are all-right ways of brainstorming, and there are great ones. Any degree of sitting-down-and-thinking-things-through is going to be a positive thing for the product, but it's possible to go through the motions and miss the meeting's full potential. So for all intents and purposes, I am going to go ahead and outline the method that, in my experience, has yielded the best results.

Scheduling matters. People seem to often be at their sharpest in the morning, if you can catch them once they're past the stage of looking like they'd blandly take a sock at anybody communicating from the World of the Awake. There's coffee (just in case), and usually juice or doughnuts or something to keep the blood sugar running right. Usually we'll let some time pass while everybody chats and settles in. After about a half an hour, though, we begin—and from ten to noon, the switch is flipped. It's two to even four solid hours of nothing but design just pounded, hammered, machine-gunned into space.

There are certain behavioral codes and parameters involved in a brainstorm, and though they're rarely brought up outright there's a wordless acknowledgment of them in the faces crowded around our meeting table. One of the primary rules is that, as far as this moment in time is concerned, there are no idiotic ideas, no stupid suggestions, not even any such thing as a spelling error when things get written on the board. Even all-in-good-fun teasing can have a very subtle implication of judgment buried somewhere in its depths, and that hint of intimidation is all that it takes to make people think twice before spitting out what's on their minds. You haven't got the time to be working in a stifled atmosphere of hesitance or caution; there needs to be an energy of genuine excitement, an enthusiasm that comes with knowing that there's not the slightest risk of being mocked. And anyway, even a 'bad' idea could inspire someone else in the room for something that's worthwhile.

Setting's also key. Most often it's best to have everyone sitting around a central conference table, where people can take down notes or scribble down thumbnail sketches for each other if they need to illustrate an idea. We work with a quiet background—the Beach Boys make great company when you're puttering in the shop, but we can't have "Help Me Rhonda" bopping around on precious neurons just right now. A good dose of clear strong light is necessary, and refreshments and whatnot should still be kept on hand to make sure we don't get anyone dying off on us any sooner than they have to. We've got a bucket full of design markers and an assortment of various pencils and pens, and for inspiration we've got what we call "mood boards," which are whole assortments full of prints or ads or magazine cutouts that show what products in this industry look like or bring to mind various intriguing mechanisms or designs.

The centerpiece to this whole mental banquet, however, is the six or eight or ten foot expanse of butcher paper tacked up on the wall. A whiteboard works just as well if you'd prefer it; for a while we used to use a giant window in our conference room with a blind pulled down behind the glass. Or it could be just a great big sheet of paper spread across a tabletop—anything really—although it's really best to have it up vertically so that everyone can see.

First of all though, it is crucial to know from the onset whether the brainstorm is A) a meeting in regards to primary content and utility (i.e. how the product operates) or B) about refining the design (the aesthetics, more or less). They are two very distinct brainstorms, and both need to happen, but the brainstorm regarding function must be covered first. For our purposes here, we'll refer to it as the Orientation Brainstorm, and this is how it goes.

Before you even start off the discussion, there are several category headings spaced across this board. At the very top, you've got the labels "PAG" and "PAU": "Problem as Given" and "Problem as Understood." PAG is essentially saying "Here's what needs to be achieved." You've been given an assignment, there's something you've got to create. PAU is in turn declaring "Here's what we understand we're supposed to do with it." It's where you're re-interpreting what you think are the goals of that assignment. The practice is somewhat of a throwback to our old consulting days; now that we have left that, the two categories might very well be one in the same. But even with the kind of work we're doing, it's almost impossible to create something with zero restrictions. There must be goals and limitations… it's just too open-ended any other way.

"Requirements" is the next heading: what the product absolutely has to do. It must be safe, for example. Or it must be, say, something that produces a result in under ten minutes. Right next to that is a more flexible category, name it what you will, of what it would be *nice* for your product to be able to do. It would be nice if it were fun, if it were intuitive and you could figure out how to do it without having to take out the directions. But these are secondary attractions. Requirements take the lead.

Next on the list are "Models &Associations." This is incredibly important; I can think of times when nearly the entire solution to a product was reached through this part of the brainstorm. The example that comes to mind at the moment was a water attraction we were once given to work on that was going to be used at the very last World's Fair. It kind of was a fun one; we were supposed to come up with some kind of a catapult where fair-goers would be able to throw water back and forth at each other across a pond. Well, we got to thinking about oceans and lakes and creeks. We thought about great big wooden parts and giant forged steel or iron pieces. We thought about a giant rubber band, or a fly swatter maybe. Colors came into the mix; if we were thinking water, well, maybe we should make it blue... It was the sort of thing that could go on and on and on.

That was "Associations." The "Models" part is always little more substantial; in this, you're looking at the existing mechanisms that can be referred to so that you're not out to reinvent the wheel. When we went to find models for our flinger, we started examining and researching the construct of actual siege engines. We looked at the mechanics of old Greek and Roman and feudalistic catapults and trebuchets; we looked even at the anatomy of the human arm. But the one that was the winner in the end was the linkage used in old-fashioned typewriters: what we ended up with was a ten-foot version of a typewriter key, in which you sat down on what was essentially the letter, and it chucked the bucket-load of water over at your friend. Consider yourself stamped.

"Processes and Materials" comes next, where, basically without stopping to think, we put down every kind of substance and every mode of production that pops into our heads. Ceramic, aluminum, plastic (it doesn't rust), vacuum forming, injection molding… We even keep a go-to list in the office printed out. It can be a very good prompt for how the product's going to look and work, not to mention how much it's going to cost.

"Details" and "Possible Solutions" are the headings after that. Keeping with the example of the catapult toy—maybe every time you sit down on the seat there's a sound effect like the lurch of an old catapult being pulled. Maybe there's a way of automatically filling up your catapult with water—or how about dying the water and having clear tubing that lets you see it being filled? As for possible solutions—maybe it's on a great big pivot so that we could point it, or there's a crank so we could figure out how far the water goes…All of these are things that we could toy with and revisit later.

I've marked off all these categories as if each one is begun and completed in a very linear manner, but the truth is that the order in which all these things are discussed is far from being orderly in any way. We might tell ourselves that we're starting with PAU and PAG and then subsequently going on to list Requirements and then neatly scooting on down to Models and so forth… But the human brain just doesn't work that way. As we go, there are going to be worthwhile ideas that pop up too early or too late, and so as we're talking we're jumping all over the place between categories, filling it all in.

Between hours two and four of brainstorming however, people are going to start to fade. We don't fight it; we bring in sandwiches or better yet we step out for a bite, we give everybody's minds a bit of time to just recharge. When we all regroup, we know the second half of the brainstorm is never going to be able to match the intensity of what the first half had been. It's just too tough to sustain that sort of thing for a full eight-hour span. So instead of trying to force it we tend to keep things pretty short and light, no more than two hours at the most. It tends to serve as a wrapping-up of sorts.

Often it's at this time that we work on our final heading, which is what we call the "Action List." The Action List is markedly different from any of the types of lists that have lead up to this point. It's at this moment that we point out the fact that we're going to need to visit a typewriter manufacturer; we're going to have to get one of us to take apart a typewriter and see how the linkage works and figure how many ways there are to make this function. It's going to be necessary to check out various materials that we could use, to look at which companies we might turn to for providing certain parts…. There are all sorts of things that after all this mulling and musing we're going to have to spring into action and achieve.

Also during this moment of reconvening when we've had our lunch and have come back to revisit it with fresh eyes, we're going to take a bright colored marker and circle all the ideas that we like so that we've in effect highlighted all the things we think we should look into or that might become action items sometime later on. Somewhere around this point, too, we make sure we have someone transcribe onto paper everything that we had written on the board.

Then it's palms down on the table, quick nod, and—Right. Let's get to work. From here on out, it's the beginning of a new phase, that period of time between the two brainstorms where every ounce of effort and attention is put towards proving and researching the ideas that before were only words flung out and slapped down onto butcher paper in black ink. It is what we sometimes call the Preliminary Model Phase: individuals going off and doing sketches, shop drawings, engineering drawings, talking to experts, researching the feasibility of different processes and materials and manufacturing techniques—seeing how difficult it would be to use a special lightweight plastic or to add on little flashing lights. All things accounted for, it amounts to an intense moment of playing inventor. And it's great.

After reviewing all the highlights of the brainstorm, we hope to end up with some rough drawings that we'll be able to promptly convert into rough working models. These models aren't meant to be precious or delicate or even fully-finished most of the time. Designers like to joke about the "clarinet reeds and bailing wire" involved during this phase, and it's true—just about anything that gets the job done is acceptable for now. These models are un-sanded, un-painted, usually mocked together out of cheap pine or anything else that lends itself to alterations more readily than steel. Essentially they are quick and dirty study models, and we're going to be putting them through the wringer with experimentation before most likely destroying them and sending them off to an eternity in mechanical Purgatory. They hardly ever get to live very long. But what we get out of them unquestionably stays. There's a whole rabble and scramble of action going on throughout this between-brainstorm period, and rather than try to muddle through linking it all in any lyrical fashion, it might be clearer to just have a cut-and-dry glossary at this point.

<u>Preliminary Model Phase Terms</u>

- Form and Volume Study
    - o This is you going and figuring out: how big does it have to be—do the handles unfold, is it the right height, where do the knee-pads go? It's addressing the question of shape and size and how the parts all fit together, as well as figuring in the human aspect of its ergonomics

and simply what feels right. I should warn you that model building is not always given due credit, as fundamental as it is. While visiting design colleges as a guest lecturer, I've had professors ask if I'd try to talk the administration out of getting rid of the school's model-building facilities, which had come to be seen as superfluous and out of date once computers came around. These were good, solid universities that specialized in design, and their students weren't learning how to make real models. The idea of schools making moves like this is horrifying. Absolutely, we can create nearly anything on a screen. But there's still no way to be certain that things fit right or feel right unless they're also being built in physical space.

○ This also might be a good moment to mention: we've got engine lathes and milling machines and welding equipment and a forge; we're really lucky with our shop. It's neither fair nor realistic, however, to presume that every innovative entrepreneur has got all this on his or her hands, or that everyone's got decades of experience in wood- and metalworking. It's a perfectly good option for someone starting up to go out and hire someone else. There are different levels you could go to; the most expensive is probably to hire an industrial designer, with the next step down being a professional model builder, and the thriftiest of all being the choice to hire someone who's still in school. That said, before you give up on the idea of doing it on your own you should keep in mind that you may have skills you haven't accounted for. I had a student once who baked a model out of dough when she was working on designing an overstuffed armchair. She didn't have a lot of knowledge about machinery and things, but she was resourceful and worked with what she knew.

- Motion Study
    - If we're designing a device that's supposed to lift something, we need to know how it's going to lift. If we're designing something like a walker, we might need to do a study not only on how tall and wide it needs to be, but on how it folds up to be stored away. Because the motion's so important, we'll usually do a specific model that focuses on motion alone, making sure that things aren't going to grind into each other or miss their aim or inadvertently chop somebody's legs off. It might sound like a big endeavor, but our average motion models are actually quite un-theatrical, and usually small enough to hold in your hand. They're almost two-dimensional, the way we make them—flat cut-outs of matte board or cardboard or plastic all cobbled together with springs, gears, rivets, rubber bands and tacks in order to make little moving arms and sliding parts. We call them "paper dolls," and

they are what allow us to very quickly test the function and produce a whole range of linkages and mechanisms. It's a technique and term relatively peculiar to our office; I wouldn't necessarily recommend going into other shops and talking about your paper dolls. But whatever you call them, they sure are good to have.

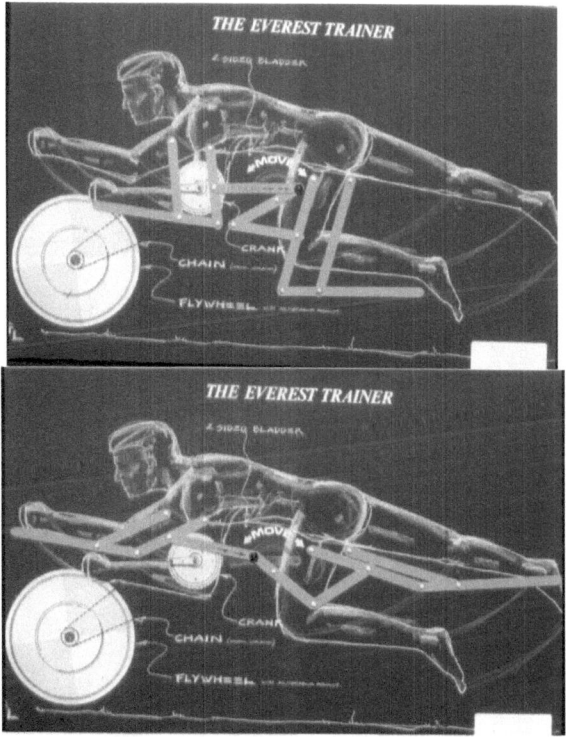

A "paper doll"

- Video/User Studies

o   When we go out and meet with professionals in our product's field, we find it's incredibly helpful to video everything we see so we can later go back and try to pick up on whatever important details we might have missed the first time around. I remember once when we were working on a film-editing machine, and, as was routine, we brought with us a small camcorder when we went to interview film editors and get the layout of their work. Although we learned a lot just in the moments we were with them, there were scores more ideas that we caught only after we played all the footage back. We noticed for example the way that with their long hours, the editors had actually been stacking mouse pads into makeshift hand-rests, or we realized how their backs were killing them from going back and forth between three different machines. After reviewing the video, we took all three machines and combined them into one, built in a hand-rest, and made it small enough so that they could do the whole thing leaning back. None of this had jumped out at us when we were there.

- Maquette
  - o You can find these going all the way back to the Renaissance, when they made small studies of big sculptures they were going to create. It's a miniature model, made out of wood or plaster or clay—a 3D sketch of what you want something to look like in the end.
- Working model
  - o A "working model" is very simply an unpolished model that is built for function and does nothing less or more than what the product is fundamentally supposed to do. From time to time you might hear the term "kluge" or "Frankenmodel" used; these are basically just more terms for the same thing. If someone says that something's kind of klugey, it means it's pretty rough

and still in the working model stage. As for Frankenmodel… well, that's just us being sort of silly I guess—it refers to the working models that are sort of mishmashes of all the previous models' best parts.

- Appearance model
  - o You could argue that the appearance model is the working model's opposite in a way. It's this wondrous little thing of beauty that's all shined up with fins and buttons and great decals—by all appearances, you could just pick it up and use it then and there. Only there's nothing in it to make it work. Sometimes we show a working model next to an appearance model at presentations just to give a better sense of the eventual consummate work.
- Rapid Prototyping
  - o When we talk about rapid prototyping we're talking about modeling that's built fairly quickly with a minimum of

tooling, if any at all. The most common forms include

- CNC Machining
  - This is where you give a machinist a computer file containing a 3D model of the product, and he basically gets a milling machine or engine lathe to cut the product out of a solid piece of material.
- SLA ("Stereolithography")
  - With SLA you've basically got a light-sensitive pool of liquid polymer and a computer-controlled laser that turns everything it touches into a solid plastic, so that by using a solid computer model you can export an STL file and in the end produce a plastic part that is within thousandths of

an inch of exactitude. It's possible to make hundreds of parts by taking silicon molds from that part and injecting them with a catalyzed plastic or resin.

- 3D Printers
  - These use an ink printer head, but instead of depositing ink they deposit layers of plastic and print a 3D model out. These days they're actually pretty affordable, considering what an incredible thing it is that they do.

By doing all this work based off of our original highlighted talking-points from the brainstorm, we may get a "Concept A" that fills our given parameters. But out of this initial concept spring new ones, and each subsequent concept becomes one step further from the last, so that by the time we get to Concept E we may often be dealing with something that's almost an entirely separate product from what we initially foresaw—and that's not a bad thing. We want a true range to choose from, one with breadth and variety of content; it's too early to be looking at five flavors of vanilla right now.[10]

Once we get to the point where we pretty much know all the mechanical components' sizes and shapes and positioning, we can begin to brainstorm an aesthetic. It's not enough that the product works well. We are working on the entirety of the creation, and for it to succeed there must be care and attention paid to every aspect, not simply the rudimentary ones. We cannot dismiss the "design" of it as being fuss and frills.

Good design is not necessarily about creating something that looks good; it's about appropriately addressing your product's goals. Right now we've got a

---

[10] If we happen to be going into production on a licensing model, then at this point we lead into the meeting with the potential licensees where we show what we've got. (*See "Presentations."*) We don't always display the same number of versions of the product; sometimes we have scores of them, sometimes only three or four. There also usually isn't just one clear "favorite" in the end—more often than not, they take elements from each, deciding for instance that they like certain aspects of one concept but wish it shared various traits belonging to the next. Assuming those qualities are not mutually exclusive, this usually amounts to us making a sort of Frankenstein monster out of all the preferences they make known.

product in the works that's supposed to be disposable. Since we knew it would be only used once and then thrown away, we went through extensive (and expensive) research seeking biodegradable materials to use. Unfortunately, we'd done just as thorough a job on the visual aspect of it—too thorough a job, in fact. Our earliest versions had the object looking sleek and streamlined; it even had a hole in the handle so that it could be hung up if need be. The product simply appeared too high-quality to ever be tossed away, and in the end we actually had to go back and ugly it up. It was a case in which we'd made the momentary error of valuing attraction over intuition, and intuition in the end is what comes first. In a world where everyone has to use up space in their brains remembering how they've programmed their iPhones, wristwatches, GPSes, laptops, and so on, it's necessary to avoid making a product any more complicated than it needs to be.

That said, we do want it to visually appeal to the user if at all possible. Cars are always a good example for how much everything comes down to looks. Given that they all do essentially the same things and for the most part get a person to work in the same amount of time, the reason for someone buying a Jaguar and not a Buick is almost entirely about design. This is true of many things. I can think of a time during the late '90s when we were hired to improve a game controller that was up against eight competitors out on the shelves. It and every other controller that it was up against were all within an eighth of an inch of the same footprint, visually interchangeable, more or less. After we'd worked on it a while, we eventually ended up with a design that was aesthetically different from the rest; it performed all of the same functions, but had a different visual feel. The result was that the product hiked from being the lowest on the list to the very first in two short months, and the manufacturers made millions. Everything came down to visual impact. It was the sole cause of that success.

Considering the often opposing natures of their aims, the Orientation Brainstorm and the Design Brainstorm are not that unalike. As before, there's an unrolled expanse of butcher paper up for everyone to see. This time, however, everyone will have his or her own personal stock of paper too, along with tracing tissue, pens, pencils, and markers close at hand. Quite often each member also is provided with his or her own full-scale skeleton of the working product shown at multiple angles and views, which will serve as a template to be sketched over using tracing paper, so that no one has to take time to figure out proportions and the like. There's a long roll of paper spread out on the conference table, where we can confer and trace over one another's sketches, but when it comes to getting an idea across, anything will do—if drawing can't convey the thought, we'll run out to the shop to do a slap-dash mock-up with glue and cardboard or a hunk of clay. In contrast with the previous brainstorm, most of this meeting's attendees will be individuals who are directly engaged in the design process. Their high-charged energy and common creative enthusiasm are what gives the Design Brainstorm the atmosphere it has.

The brainstorm begins with us essentially reiterating what we highlighted in the prior discussion and posting it up where everyone can see. Just as before, our second meeting will have a sheaf of butcher paper filled with headings for various lists. The first among them is a list of Requirements, and it's while focusing on this heading that, among other things, we take a moment to consider the identity of the consumers. We need to take into consideration the consumer's age, their generation even, their subculture if subcultures come into play. It's important to have an idea of what gender we're working with, since that can affect everything from the product's color to its architecture to its name, and it matters that we know what economic bracket the consumer falls into, since helps us determine the product's perceived value (i.e. what impression it gives of its monetary worth).

Models might not really come up again this time around, but Associations definitely do. We'll say for a moment that you have an aromatherapy product that you are working on. The whole topic of aromatherapy might have you thinking along the lines of something Zen, which might make your mind turn to Japan, which leads you to start mulling over all different types of bamboo, maybe— which in turn brings you to smooth textures and yellows and greens... Whatever the product might be, a whole tree of associations is built up the moment these connections begin. Detail-snapshots and magazine clippings are pinned up onto the board; usually we'll make an inspiration list of products with a similar feel. Quite often they are objects that aren't directly related to the product at hand—a hairdryer might not seem to have any pertinence to the kitchen appliance you're designing, but we are thinking in the world of aesthetics now, and utility parallels are the last thing on our minds. You look at styles, and decide if you're going for a sort of a Porsche thing or instead more of a Jeep look—or maybe an Apple style, or something a little more steam-punk or postmodern or traditional in its appeal. It helps at this point-of-a-million-options that there are definite parameters and limitations defined for you by the material you'll be using, something that you have likely already decided on by now.

Once there's this full spread of information, it's time to mix and match. In the combination stage, we might look at the prospect of a concept that A) is made from ceramic, B) has the look of a Cadillac, and C) is blue... Or—wait, shoot, let's go back—maybe it's red! The combinations are almost infinite.

From there we let the designers go off to private corners with their tracing paper and their sketching gear, and they're allotted a set amount of time to tear through as many new renditions as they can. At the end of it, everybody slaps their work up on the wall. As person by person gives an orientation on what they came up with, it brings up all sorts of new ideas, a whole new stage of refinements. There are people with lucky misunderstandings, people with light bulbs going off jumping in at lulls to sketch in new additions... Occasionally we may get everyone to return to their corners for a second round to fine-tune things, and then once again: more ideas come about.

After that there's a certain Distillation process, in which we sort the artwork out into four or five categories, deciding—here are all the sort of "high tech" ones that we like, here's where we've got our favorite post-modern looks in case we end up going for that type of thing instead, here are the best of the military-type designs, or the best sophisticated ones, and so forth and so on. This isn't the full "design" process in itself, but it is a part of it; it's the styling phase. When it finally gets to a point where we've pinpointed all the best elements we've got, we send our designers out to explore one or all of these directions, and the almighty brainstorm ends, only to be followed with another, tighter, presentation after days or weeks of work.

For any creative mind, however, there are going to be moments of creative "block." When I was briefly a staff designer in a consulting firm there were for long periods of time when we might be on task to bring a sense of style to intensely basic objects—designing, say, a Bluebonnet margarine container over the course of a month. Well, it doesn't take long to realize your soul only has so many Bluebonnet margarine containers in it. Out of desperation then, we'd turn to what I like to call "dry hole techniques"— quick-cheats to overcoming a creative block.

There used to be a show on television when I was a kid, a sort of Popeye program or something along those lines, where the host would do a demo for the kids by making a blindfolded scribble and then reworking it into some kind of cartoon. When it comes to margarine containers—or any other mind-numbingly uninspiring object you find yourself trying to design—this nice little parlor-trick stops being just for kicks-and-giggles and becomes a grown-up concept-generating tool. You sit down. You make a mental contract with yourself that you'll follow through, and you make a squiggle on the page. Then, no matter what the hell kind of mess it looks like, you are going to turn that thing into a plastic butter dish.

Or instead of doing squiggles, you might find yourself going through books and magazines for new associations and ideas—you might page through them upside down. You might pull cards, pre-written: one that might tell you to come up with three ideas and design the second one, another that might give you the prompt to design something that you hate, the third maybe instructing you to create a design just the way your best friend would do it, or to do one based on a platypus, or to make it art nouveau.

If all else fails, there's always sleep. There are times when I potentially could work till four a.m. and still leave empty-handed, but once I've walked away to give my mind a chance to breathe, I suddenly am rushing back with something new that must be jotted down. Sometimes the biggest hurdle to creativity is looking just too long and close.

—

Processes and Materials

There is no way for this to be a thorough chapter. The subject of processes and materials is a whole university degree unto itself, and with this in mind, I will not even going to begin to attempt to convey everything that needs to be known about plastics and composites and factory processes and so forth. That said, there are a few rudimentary ideas that the reader ought to be informed of.

When we talk about processes and materials, we're essentially talking about what your product is made out of and which methods are used to make it. Those may seem like two totally isolated decisions, but the processes that are used are very much dependent on which materials are chosen, and same truth follows for the other way around. If you were to simply pick your favorite material and your favorite manner of manufacturing without taking into account that the two would have to work in accordance with each other's limitations, then, unless there were some very slim-slice-on-the-probability-pie-chart accident-of-fate, you'd be (ohhhhhh manufacturing pun—) screwed.

The variety of available design processes is highly extensive. There's the injection-molding of plastic, the forging of steel, the stamping of brass, the weaving of fibers, the blowing of glass—each process, whatever it might be, has certain very exact materials that can be used. For example, with injection molding we may choose to use plastic—but not all plastics are moldable in the same way. Every process has its rules, almost like that of a game. Carrying on with our example of molding plastic parts—the mold must employ radii at its edges and have a certain amount of taper (draft) in order to eject the form. There are rules-of-the-trade involved in every process there is.

Just as the list of potential processes goes on and on, so too does the list of materials. You've got your stone, your plaster, your concrete; there's clay, glass, leather, fabric, rope, webbing, bamboo, wood, steel, copper, aluminum... the roll call never ends. Naturally, every one of these materials carries with it its own "cans" and "cannots," its own advantages and disadvantages depending on its use. Some materials float, some sink; some are clear, others are opaque. Often there are hugely differing properties even within the same category of material. If you wanted to make a bullet proof door you could use polycarbonate, which is literally bullet proof plastic, while another plastic like ABS might be great for telephone housing but would stand up terribly against a

Colt. The same goes for metals, for textiles, for different types of glasses and woods. In design school we used to joke about Unobtainium, this ideal all-encompassing material that did whatever you wanted it to do. If you needed it to be bulletproof, if you needed it to bounce, if you needed it to have the texture of an overused Muppet— maybe all three all at once— then, well shoot, Unobtainium was the material for you. Unfortunately, it's got one small disadvantage, and it's right there in its name.

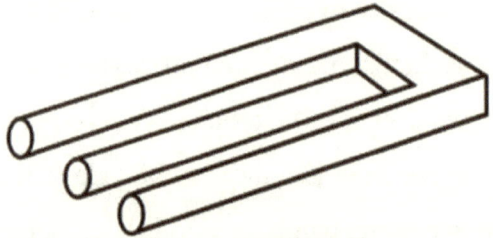

Just because you can visualize something doesn't mean you can make it physically work

One thing that is important to recognize is that different processes and materials go hand and hand with different volumes of manufacturing, and so when choosing manufacturing methods it's best to keep the production-run in mind. An injection mold (to keep running with that example) is very expensive; just to make the mold itself costs high into the thousands, so I am not going to make much of a profit using an injection mold if I only need it for one hundred copies. The same is true the other way around. If I wanted to make just a hundred of something— maybe a very high-end product that was going to be in limited production— then certainly, it would be very easy for me to go ahead and have it hand-carved by little old men hard at work somewhere deep in the Black Forest. But if I want to have it done in the hundreds of thousands, in the millions, I'm not going to go out and enlist an entire army of elderly German woodworkers. Not by a long shot.

If you're looking to gain a more thorough knowledge on the subject of processes and materials, there are ways to teach yourself. There are some very good books available—there's *The Materials Handbook*, which was written roughly at the same time as the Book of Genesis, and an excellent series titled *The Way Things Work* that scores of people have found helpful through the years.

It's possible, however, that in addition to (or perhaps even instead of) manically working to educate yourself on everything there is to be known, you'll find there's some wisdom in taking on help— from an uncle, a neighbor, a good friend… It could be anyone, so long as they know how things go together and understand how to deal with the reality that all processes and all materials have benefits and limitations and rules. Of course, there's also the somewhat more reliable (albeit more costly) option of hiring an engineering student or an industrial designer to do the work—but whoever it is, I would encourage you to utilize everything they have to offer, and to consider possibly even bringing them to the presentation meeting as well.

I don't think we'll beat it to death... But be sensitive to the fact that this is a product that is going to have to actually be built, with real physics, by real people and machines.

For a cursory list of commonly used processes and materials, see the processes and materials listings at the end of the text.

—

Organized Minds:

The Three-Percenters

There was a period for about twenty years when I used to teach and study martial arts, and during that time there was something odd that would catch my attention as I watched students come and go. Out of every hundred white belts that started off brand new, probably only about three ever came to be a black belt. Out of a hundred first degree black belts, I could always reckon that only about three percent of those ever would ever go on to their second degrees, and out of those three percent only about three percent of *those* ever got their third.

Years later, there was a study done at one of the major Ivy Leagues that seemed to be very much tied to this same phenomenon. Researchers took a sampling of a hundred brand-new students and examined their daily habits in an attempt to identify the genuine planners, and in spite of the indubitable abundance of intelligence within the pool, there were only three who really fit the hard-core "planner" bill. Now, I will be among the first to say that assessments can't be made based on how much money is involved—but for our purposes here, it's at least a quantifiable way of looking at things. In short, when the researchers went back to see what had become of their subjects a few years down the line, the three people whom they had identified as planners not only came out to be the most financially successful of the group, but the very sum of their three lone incomes exceeded the net worth of the other ninety-seven combined.

I don't like to bash the whimsy and romance of the classic innovator stereotype—I as much as anyone love the idea of the scatter-brained inventor with spring-coils on his head, shocking the village with his brilliance in spite of all his absentminded ways. But in licensing, just as much as in any other field, there really is a need to be serious about organization. *We* must *be* the three-percenters; it makes every bit as much of a difference in a design shop as it does a martial arts studio or a university hall.

Obviously, there are various tools that assist in this. We've already talked about binders and totes—in addition to this (and at the risk of sounding like your junior high school guidance counselor) I would like to put in a word for calendars….. For anyone who's not naturally inclined to use them, it's going to become more vital than ever once you enter into the licensing process, and the sooner you can start, the faster you'll be on your way.

Partly, it's for legal purposes; you're going to want to have a daily record breaking the day down into fifteen minute increments with the jobs are numbered and the activities coded, so that you can look at any particular month and know exactly how much time you spent on any specific project.

This is the recording side of it— making sure you know just what occurred and when. But equally important is the planning. By your usage of your datebook you have ensured yourself a disciplined log of deadlines—when something must be finished, when a fee needs to be paid, when your patent might expire or on which dates your clients wish to meet. You maintain your accountability in this way; you're more likely to be on beat with everybody else.

But what's every bit as vital is that by dealing with deadlines, you are in effect taking an overwhelming project and breaking it up into tiny manageable steps. As an innovator you might be working on anything from a toy to a new medical project within the same year. You might be working with subjects with which you have never had any experience before, projects that never existed before, and if you're going to make anything come of it you need to go about it in a fairly quick and efficient manner.

Back when I was in my professorship, it was a customary requirement for students in their third year of furniture design to have to come up with their first chair. This usually was the first really overwhelming project for them. It wasn't only that it dealt with styling; it dealt with ergonomics, with different kinds of fabrication, different kinds of finishing and assembly techniques.

Usually what I would say to them at this point was— first— sit down, get out your drafting gear, let's get your design done. Well, okay. Once we've got a design that we like—well, why don't we blow it up full scale; let's make a front view and a side view and a top view while we're at it. All right, that's that. Well, then once you've done that, do you know what kind of material you're going to use? How much of it will you need?... Okay, we've figured that out. Well, let's take your drawings and let's lay out each part individually; how's it going to be cut or welded or bent....

A large-scope project, when taken as a whole and not as a composite, can be enough to make any designer want to sit down on the floor of the shop, stare into space, and hug their knees as they rock back and forth. But by breaking it up into these small steps and small successes, things happen. In the end, the student always had a finished chair.

Enlisting Help

There is a regrettably accurate stereotype out there that essentially sums up to this: when it comes to doing business, most creative people are a little slow. Not slow in the cautious sense; we aren't talking about pace. The suffix "-witted" comes to mind.

Most industrial designers seem to meet this fact with generally good-humored self-deprecation. Somewhere beneath that thin veneer, however, I suspect there is usually a certain bizarre pride, a sense of camaraderie— a slightly smug belief that our deal-making and figure-managing ineptitudes are somehow inversely proportionate with our creative knack. And then beneath this pride, there is yet another layer to be found: one of sheer panic that no amount of self-beguilement in our own da Vinci-esque eccentricity ever will console.

And so in the end, we shake the hands of the nice, levelheaded accountants in the pinstriped suits, leave their (aesthetically flawed and ergonomically inaccurate) office chairs, and pinch the bridges of our noses with the thought that although these men would never make it as designers, neither will we (professionally, at least) without some outside help.

The fact is that the whole business of learning to do business is inexpressibly inconvenient for most people of the design mold. But before we start stabbing bitterly at the "too much" that's on our plates, it might help to remember that there is no rule that says that we personally are the ones to have to tackle it. The earlier you identify your weak points and subsequently hand them over to someone else to deal with—someone who specializes in those specific areas himself—then the faster the creative side of things will be able to evolve into something real. Moreover, you'll be that much freer to turn your focus towards the things at which you do excel—and, frankly, which you probably enjoy the most as well.

There are several different categories that the members of your network are going to fall into. The first, chronologically at least, is the start-up guru. Whatever it might take to get a business going, it's something he knows how to do. Financiers are incredibly important as well; you might be working with venture capital groups, for instance, or you might have "angels," as we like to call any given individuals who are interested in loaning or investing money in the designer's pursuit. Attorneys are extremely important to have on hand too; because of the nature of licensing, we hire one who specializes just in that, and we are able to benefit greatly from his specific knowledge of the infomercial world.

If your focus is manufacturing, and if for theory's sake there had to be just one person who you were able to get onto your team, it might be a CEO or MBA. If your focus is specifically licensing, it might be a broker.

There needs to be somebody to help you locate potential licensees. Brokers, in the design world at least, cover all their own expenses. When they meet with us it's not necessary for us personally to fly them out here, because more often than not they are in the area for purposes of their own, often to meet for unrelated business with the very manufacturing firms with which we would like to be put into contact. To assemble a network of brokers takes some time, but having one—or even possibly several who are active in different industries—can be a huge asset for a designer who otherwise would have had a hard time getting through the front door to make a presentation.[11]

---

[11] One thing I should mention in regards to this whole symbiotic relationship is that, as a company, we are firm on the fact that we don't give our brokers exclusives. Even though we don't want to have to act as our own brokers, the ability to have an "out" is a huge freedom for us in our work. It's necessary to leave ourselves in a

Innovators are not the only ones who benefit from this relationship. If the product that the broker helps present in fact turns out to be a hit, the innovator becomes the broker's asset. Because of the innovator, the broker gains a heightened credibility and perceived value among his clients, not to mention the advantage of being linked to any future jobs that are born out of the product that he helps us get produced. There is also an opportunity for him to have a certain direct share in the profits: When a broker not only sets us up with clients but also remains actively involved in our communications with them over time, that broker often may enjoy a percentage of that product's royalties—an incentive if there ever was one when it comes connecting us with licensees.

Sometimes you might find the help you need not in an individual but in an organization. We've most recently been reminded of this through our meetings with SCORE Association, a nonprofit supported by the U.S. Small Business Association whose purpose is to assist small businesses. Through the volunteer mentors at SCORE, we have been able to receive not only counseling on the writing up of our business plan, but assistance in connecting with everyone from business and marketing

position where we have options.

professionals to funding-sources. There are no contracts, no shares. It's just collaboration, and it works.

But while we're on the topic of different types of outside help, a quick world about inventors' services.

Don't do it.

Kits, services, 'let-us-help-you-make-a-quick-buck' type-firms—we do not recommend this path, even as a last resort. The truth is that the vast majority of these companies are incredibly difficult to get straight answers from regarding the details of their deals, and although it's hard to place an exact number on the percentage of customers that actually wind up with successful licenses from them, it's understood to by-and-large be something very rare.

There may be some great inventor services out there. We just haven't found many yet. (Well. *Any* yet.) So for the time being, we will go ahead and say that turning to these companies is roughly tantamount to the scene where the scraggly-bearded, lazy-eyed peddler stops the hero on the road and sells him the suspicious-looking potion that fouls up every single aspect of the plot. It's the equivalent of getting excited over the weird messages sent to your phone that assure you "you're the winner!"; it would be like very seriously researching a palm-reader's credentials so you can go to them for advice in your career. With due respect to all the peddlers, psychics, and cell-phone con artists that might indignantly be reading this right now—better just to leave it alone.

—

Funding

The advice of business gurus generally seems to be against risking one's own money, and in favor of getting other people to invest. There must be something to that, if that's the conventional wisdom, but personally I like the idea of self-funding. I think I'd feel more secure in taking that method and being a little bit poorer for it than I would in having ample funds but always wondering how to answer to investors the next day.

I'll admit that it can be a little dicey to do things independently when one is "bootstrapping it" financially. It's possible to try asking at the bank… but it's very unlikely for a small inventor to be able to walk out with an unsecured loan. It's possible to take out a second mortgage on one's house, but that comes with its own full set of disadvantages. Of course, there is the option of using credit lines and credit cards; The Bank of Visa, I like to call it. People do it; I have done it in the past. But the last time I did, it was only due to luck that we were able to scrape by: in that last month before we began receiving royalties, we'd used up three credit lines and every credit card and had absolutely nothing left. It's an option, certainly, but this whole concept that the cavalry is going to get there just in the nick of time just ain't true most of the time.

However, there are some independent methods that feel a little less like loading one sixth of your chambers and giving them a spin.

There are Angels, aptly-named. We've talked about angels a little before—essentially, an "angel" can be a friend of the family, a family member, a friend of a friend; they're the investors-from-anywhere who put money into the project and in turn have some degree of equity in the company or profits or else just simple paid interest. The trouble is that in any of these cases a friendship is a fragile thing and a business is risky one, and it's a drawback worth keeping in mind.

There are investment breakfast clubs available, in which people meet as groups to discuss potential investment prospects, so one possibility could always be to track down one of these and request to present to them. Or, another good place to find willing and able providers— there are what they call "inventors' conventions," which are essentially bazaars put on by DR companies where they have booths available for people with new products. From time to time they'll even get inventors up in front of cameras to spread the news about their work; you really couldn't ask for a better platform for your product, as long as you don't get caught up making connections with some kind of a shark.

There are also civic and government-sponsored economic development centers, where volunteers can either connect you with funding or can offer their expertise on things like writing out a business plan. The United States Small Business Administration (www.sba.gov) is always a good place to go for financial assistance. There are also all sorts of grants to be had, of course; they've got them for people who are involved in medical products or energy-based products or products based in transportation... It's not a fast process or a simple one; you'll have to write a proposal and then go through different levels of evaluation. But if it does go through a grant will provide some critical funding.

When it comes to independent funding, however, sometimes the best methods are the ones that are so simple that they're almost in danger of being overlooked. There is something to be said for that basic feudalistic idea of just trading services, means, or skills. Maybe you've got yourself a neighbor who is a decent machinist, or a nephew who can weld. There's nothing out there that says it has to be any more complicated than that. University scholars are also a fantastic tool. Walk into any faculty office at the local college, ask about grad students or undergrads that might be interested in being offered a part in your project, either as an internship or as work experience that's paid; you'll find there are plenty of takers to be had. Naturally, you'll get a student's work, not a professional's, but some of these young students are in fact incredibly good at what they're learning to do. On a similar note at the opposite extreme, you could find your greatest asset not among the youths but with the retirees. Whole organizations exist of former executives who are willing to lend their time and assistance to those who are just starting out, and their mentorship about career paths and financial decisions could be the foundation for your career.

Now, you probably know that there are different types of corporations based on whether or not investors are involved. There are "S" Corporations, which are small businesses, but since the taxes roll through to "personal" in this system, an S Corporation probably isn't the right format for someone with investors on their hands. One format that *does* have investors is the "C Corporation," but those tend to be fairly large established companies with high-cost bookkeeping. All is not lost, however. Keep in mind that there are still "limited liability companies"

(LLC's) which are their own sort of beast and not a corporation at all really, and which could be just the thing for investment-gathering entrepreneurs who are beginning small.

As we've long-since established in this text, the standard manner of manufacturing for designers who license is for the product to be licensed to the manufacturers (i.e. licensees) who pay for everything— tooling and inventory and packaging and any other marketing or production costs. And although this is the typical way of getting things done, it's not the only one.

As we have discussed earlier, there is such a thing as self-manufacturing, in which the designer himself is in charge of the production, without the help of a manufacturing firm. Self-manufacturing doesn't necessarily mean having to build factories. When we have done it in the past, we've had nearly all activities outsourced. Assuming you can afford the tooling and the inventory, along with the warehousing and shipping and the rest, you can in fact find and hire companies to make the products' parts for you. They send you the inventory, which you own, and whether or not you are physically overseeing the manufacturing yourself, you're still the manufacturer by virtue of the fact that the funding comes from you.

When it comes to actually selling self-manufactured goods, there are a couple of options available. You could A) sell it on your own in the off-the-tailgate sense, which is a perfectly legitimate means, B) sell it through the internet, whether through professional web-designers or fully on your own, or C) license it to an infomercial company or any other marketing licensee that will help you make a royalty off of manufacturing[12]—you could even just sell it to them wholesale and leave it all in their hands from there. It's possible that you may be able to get both a wholesale price for it and have royalties on top of that, you never know— but whatever you're doing, you want to make sure you're getting enough back that you don't end up manufacturing for free. "Option C" is nice in some ways and not in others; going down that road takes a lot of responsibility off of you and will probably give your product greater reach and visibility, but keep in mind that the product gets marked up in price every time it goes through someone else's hands, and you in turn get just a little less.

---

[12]If they want exclusivity, then you might in addition to selling them the product get a royalty (or compensation of some sort) on top of that… You don't just give that away.

Also... an 'aside.' We've referred before to this idea of "keeping your day job," of not becoming so eager that you prematurely abandon your original living in order to put everything towards The Dream. I know that it sounds very smirking and skeptical for me to sit here from the comfort of my own long-realized aspirations and tell you not to be overly convinced of yours. But the truth of the matter is that during those early years of ours, our design consulting firm was the one safety net that allowed us to tend to the business of starting up our new licensing firm with any amount of responsibility or security. Or food. We worked all the normal hours of all our normal work, as if we had nothing else going on, and in our between time we did what needed to be done in order to get our new licensing business to an independent point. Eventually we did get to where we could close the consultancy down altogether, but the old firm had always been what was used to fund the new firm's projects until then. So even though it might be tempting to cast away those safety nets, to make some all-or-nothing, do-or-die decision that will force you Never To Back Down, there's something to be said for maintaining a certain grounded sense of prudence—or of humility even, if I could be

permitted to use the word— as you move forward with
your plans.

—

Nondisclosure Agreements: How to Keep Your Mouth Shut

(And Keep a Hand Clamped over Everybody Else's Too)

They say that everybody loves a secret. When it comes to hearing secrets, maybe this is true. Keeping them, however, would appear to be another story—nobody enjoys having to hold onto any worthwhile piece of knowledge for any substantial period of time. Nonetheless, a part of the licensing methodology I'm going to address is non-disclosure agreements—contracts designed to control who does or does not know about a product during the early days when it still is vulnerable to being stolen away. As the project comes to be a bigger and bigger part of your life, it can be difficult not to bring it up—certainly at least, there's something unthinkable about responding to anyone's friendly curiosity with some version of "It's a seeecret, I can't saay!"

But it pretty much is a secret. And you pretty much can't say. Because even though it can be somewhat socially painful to be so guarded in what you do or don't disclose, there's just too much at stake.

For one thing, there's just the basic problem of simple slip-ups. Say you just-this-once tell someone "safe," who himself might just-this-once tell another someone "safe" who might in turn be overheard by someone not-at-all-so-"safe" when it comes up in conversation at a coffee shop somewhere down the line. Or there are well-intentioned misunderstandings. Imagine for example that a cousin of yours wants to get you to tell her more about what you've been up to with this new product that she keeps hearing you're working on. You begin to tell her a bit about it, and she exclaims—"Oh! You should add little blinking lights to it." "Well," you try to explain, "we *have* talked about that a lot—it's definitely a possibility, we've been thinking that we actually might..." You visit, you toy with different ideas; it's a pleasant little exchange. But when you roll out your product in another year or two, you've suddenly got a passive-aggressive relative cornering you at the next family reunion and saying—"Hey! I told you about the blinking lights, and you cut me out of the deal..."

All in all, it's best to talk in broad generalities where friends and family are concerned. You don't want to kill the mood of the Christmas party by flourishing out some long legal scroll for them to sign, but you really can't

129

afford to wear your design on your sleeve, so to speak. If you need it, there's always the excuse that you're not legally allowed to disclose the details of your product to anyone while you are without a provisional patent or patent pending. And it's true: by law you technically cannot file for a patent once the product has been publicly exposed or spoken about.[13]

If things can get this itchy even when dealing with family and friends, it goes without saying that when it comes to prospective licensees, non-disclosure agreements are a must. There are several loopholes to the secrecy in these situations, involving instances where there are products that the licensee was already working on or had had brought to them by persons with legal rights to them, or circumstances involving ideas that have at some point become part of the public domain. But in nearly any other case, it is imperative to guard one's project with discerning care. Because as I've said before, if you have a good product, you will most likely begin to have people edging in on your success.

---

[13] More than anything, this rule is true of moments where the discussion has the purpose of interesting somebody in the product's license or its sale. For our purposes here though, we'll stick with the technicalities and won't get caught up on that particular nuance.

There are several crucial elements that must go into a good non-disclosure contract. Firstly, the parties must be identified. There are unilateral NDAs, where you as the innovator are having the licensees agree to keep the secret, and then there are mutual NDAs, where both parties are bound. Occasionally I do scratch my head a little at how we on the innovating side could ever break a contract like this even if we tried, seeing as the licensees don't in fact have any secret for us to even keep, but you can't blame them for wanting to play it on the safe side.

Simple as it seems, exactitude regarding the subject of the secrecy is all too often overlooked—half the NDA's I get don't name the product that they were written about. The marketing company might not take issue with such vagueness when they sign on the line, but if things come to a head, you can't show an agreement like that to a judge or an attorney and expect to have them back you up. It needn't be an issue; all you have to do is name the object at stake and broadly describe it. But it is one of your first priorities in all of this.

Signatures seem like they would naturally be the most mindless part of the whole deal, but it requires a little more carefulness than that. Is he signing it as David Smith, or as David Smith of Such-and-Such Inc.? You are going to want the company to be in the document, even down to their address.

The date and term must be listed, telling when the period of discretion begins and for how long it will last. The lengths vary from firm to firm, but at Splane Design we make a point of maintaining the right to insist on confidentiality without an expiration date. The way we see it, a secret is a secret, done and sealed, the end. When people tell each other secrets in real life, they either give their word to protect the secrecy of the matter, or else they warn it might not be something they want the responsibility for. There is never a question of "Well, um, listen, what if I keep my mouth shut for the next two-point-five years?" Furthermore, when it comes to business, it's simply hard to manage any kind of file or calendar of who promised five years and who said ten, whose term is up and who's still on their oath. On a few very rare occasions, we do agree to a time limit, but even then we draw the line at five years at the least. Negotiating on anything less than that would simply go against all common sense, because the fact is that if someone came and offered us a non-disclosure agreement that spanned two years and we were to file for a patent even the very next day, that patent would literally not even have a chance to be issued before the expiration of their term.

There are a couple of other extra stipulations that we add to our agreements at Splane Design. One is that if we are disclosing our work with prospective licensees who turn out to be working on a highly similar product, they have to come back and inform us within five to ten days, not a year or two down the line. Another difference is that our contract prevents licensees from reverse engineering— they can't find out how the product works and then design one of their own in such a way that they circumvent the patent. Since these stipulations aren't universally made in the world of design and aren't always anticipated, sometimes we have to add them into the suggested contracts that are sent to us. For the most part, however, these alterations are seen to be minor mandates and don't slow down the process all too much.

There will always be those who regrettably will refuse to sign an NDA, but it nevertheless is a demand we feel we have to make. On a couple of rare occasions we have made compromises to this hard-and-fast rule (assuming we at least had a provisional patent or a patent pending) but all in all, even in the moments when we are already in the patent office and are fully and lawfully protected—even when legally we could easily show our product without any sort of NDA—we almost always still try to get one just for safety's sake. Better to be too careful than to risk losing it all over one avoidable mistake.

—

If You Do Decide to License

The "Ideal" Infomercial Product

This is by no means meant to be taken as a hard-and-fast list of every quality that the product absolutely has to have. But if at all possible, the *ideal* product is one that:

- **Demonstrates well on TV**
  - o It's something you can see and understand and generally just get excited about when you watch. If it tells a good story and lends itself to fervent rabble-rousing testimonials, all the better.
- **Solves a problem**
  - o This, in a way, goes hand-in-hand with the bullet-point above: the best is when the dilemma that the product addresses makes John Doe nod at the television screen and remark, "Ah God, that happens to me all the time—d'you ever get that too, where you just can't get the thing to pull up/plug in/lock tight/pour

135

right..." Every day all of us mindlessly run into specific nagging difficulties that we put up with because we never step back to think about finding a clever way around them. Identifying these simply takes a certain amount of awareness, and addressing them doesn't need to be anything mind-blowingly complex. I always think back to that scene in *The Great Escape* where the prisoners-of-war sit meticulously planning their highly advanced tunnel operations. They've got pulleys, they've got five-foot long air pumps, they've got yards of cable and electric wires. When Steve McQueen wanders in with his own off-the-cuff idea for a slap-dash two-man burrow, they're skeptical. How does he propose to breathe? McQueen waves it off: he's got a collapsible rod to poke little holes into the tunnel's ceiling as he goes. He grins and shrugs and bops out of the room with his coffee cup, and there's a hung-over beat of silence among the blank faces of the other men. "Now, why hasn't anybody thought of that before?" someone finally says. "It's so *stupidly simple*, it's positively brilliant."

- **Is unique**
    - o Having a memorable product that stands apart as something different is a big deal; it narrows down the competition by a heap. It's a frequent enough circumstance for people to look at an infomercial and say, "I need to keep my eye out for something kind of like that." Preferable by far though is the product that makes them say—"I need *that*. And I know I'm not going to run into it anywhere else."

- **Can be "married" with a celebrity, an image, or a name**
    - o This pertains specifically to licensing for the infomercial world. Some D.R. companies really like products that can be connected in some way to a popular public figure, whether it be Gene

Simmons or Jean Simmons; sometimes there will even be instances when the link is made with a particular company that specializes in what the product is for (e.g.—being affiliated with Yankee Candle when selling something that clips onto a dashboard to emit scents). If you're going to go this way, finding the right fit for the image that you're aiming to sell really is essential.

- **Is safe**
  - o You'll never be at a place where there is "no" potential for lawsuits or returns, but you want to get as close to it as you can. Pinch points, sharp edges, wires that can electrocute you, what have you. Get rid of them.

- **Works well**
  - o This shouldn't really have to be listed here—it goes without saying that the dignity of any designer rests on the attention he gives to the quality of what he creates. However ridiculous the product might be, it should at least have

the decency to *work*. If this weren't a good enough reason unto itself, the aforementioned threat of false claims lawsuits and returns (especially in this age of internet reviews) should serve as an additional motive to keep your products honest and dependable and clean. There are a lot of companies that try to find ways to make a lot of money with products that are cheap and don't work. I personally don't believe in it, ethically or fiscally.

- **Is appropriate for high volume**
  - This is another one that is specific to licensing to infomercial companies, whose the goal is to sell products that are capable of being manufactured either in tens or hundreds of thousands or even in the millions.
- **Is easily stored and transported and can offer "no assembly required"**
  - These are actually fairly effective qualities, as simple as they seem. If at all possible, you want a product that

comes all folded down and is ready to pop up into full form without much of a to-do, something with a carry case that fits under the bed, and so on. It's not just for the sake of the consumer—in licensing situations, many a licensee has thrown in the towel on a project simply because it just wasn't worth the money that would be needed in order to ship the bulky crates from China to the USA.

- **Is easily manufactured**
  - Is it a product that can be made at high volume? And does it have a fairly affordable cost of manufacture in spite of its high perceived value? There's a term called "shoot-and-ship" that is used from time to time to describe products that can be manufactured quickly and easily because they use common materials and processes. It's a bit of a hassle when you're dealing with a complex manufacturing process no one's willing to perform, although it must be said that a hard-to-source process (or a

process of your own creation) can in some ways be a blessing, at least in the sense that it's yet another barrier for competitors trying to counterfeit your work or knock you off. That actually leads us to our next bullet-point...

- **Is difficult to knock off**
  - o On one of our most recent products we ended up actually losing half our profits to all the counterfeits and knockoffs that cropped up after its success. We'll go deeper into talking about patenting and trademarks in a bit, but for now just know that as long as competitive trickiness is a part of this industry, you've simply got to have some mechanisms for slowing that greed down. Your product should be of a nature that you are able to guard it through whatever means you have.

- **Fits into an ideal selling price**
  - o Particularly if you happen to be dealing with the infomercial business, there are different standard price points by which

products are advertised. Short-form commercials, which run just under three minutes, will have products running at $9.95 or $19.95. Longer air time, usually fitting into thirty-minute slots, usually corresponds with pricier products whether they be $39.95, $99.95. $199.95, or more. (Interestingly, the condescension of the ".95" trap never seems to do due damage to the sales…) The option of making multiple payments often is offered in more costly cases, where people might feel intimidated or extravagant paying the whole sum all at once.[14]

- **Has low-cost manufacturing, high perceived value**
    o Because of how expensive it is just to buy TV time, most of the companies you license to are going to want something

---

[14]Whether you decide to go for a short-form infomercial or a long-form one really should depend on what kind of a product you're working with—don't just base your decision on the fact that short-form advertising is less costly to have done. If you've got a pricy product or one that requires some convincing, long-form is the choice for you.

that can be marked up by maybe four to six times its manufacturing cost so that a worthwhile profit can be made. As consumers, this is bound to make us wince ("I'll be damned if it cost anywhere near $19.99 to injection-mold that thing…"), but as designers we swallow it as part of the trade.

- **Lends itself to "continuity sales"**
  - o It's a major asset to be dealing with a product that is not a one-sale deal. Vitamins and skin-care products, cleaning agents, makeup—all of these are a hit with infomercial companies because they naturally necessitate reordering, or possibly even subscribing for regularly-scheduled replacements to come in through the mail. By extension, the same attitude applies to products that lend themselves to a string of accessories: if your product is a sporty close-shave razor, the fact that there is now the issue of disposable razor blades to go with them is not to be dismissed.

- **Is eco-friendly**
  - o Being composed of biodegradable or otherwise "green" materials is a definite plus for a product, especially considering how many of today's products are disposable. An eco-friendly product helps the buyer feel good about what they're buying, and it definitely makes us feel better about what we do.

That more or less caps it off—but when all is said and done, keep in mind that none of these individual qualifications are anything more than just ideals. I'd hate to have anyone stop themselves from coming out with what genuinely is a worthwhile product simply because they're worried about it not fitting every one of the supposed prerequisites that's listed above. The main ideal is still a solid, worthwhile product that is worth putting your name on and is worthy of people's hard-earned pay.

—

Presentations

Presentations are ubiquitous in business, and the majority of the advice that I'm about to delineate is advice that can be applied to consulting, licensing, self-manufacturing, and most any kind of other business model that exists within design. But because making presentations is specifically crucial in licensing, it might be best to approach it from a licensing point of view.

In the early stages of prospective licensee expressing interest in a product, there is an exchange in which we send them a deal summary. Instead of sending them the twenty-page license itself, we send a one-page summary of what we are looking for in a deal. As succinctly as possible, the document covers whether we are asking for exclusive or limited rights, whether or not there will be an upfront fee, whether or not they will have ownership of the model, sketches, and computer files,[15] how much of a royalty we are going to negotiate, and so forth. It details our expectations about all of the major milestones: how promptly we anticipate proof that they have done a preproduction prototype or have filed for patents in our name for example, or how soon they have to

_____

[15] Without stipulations about these materials being sent back, we often would have to recreate models and sketches and files repeatedly after lending them out to be reviewed.

have purchased tooling, shot the commercial, and rolled out the product itself (usually around a year).

Essentially, it's a litmus test of sorts; it helps us to easily identify how close we are in wanting the same things out of an agreement. If there's too much of a difference of opinion, we drop it. There are a lot of small failures to be suffered just by the nature of the industry, and it's important to learn to get past those failures systematically.

It's difficult, however, to present potential licensees with an executive summary right off the bat. We've tried doing it, but it's a bit like trying to get someone to buy a car when all they know about it is the price. Furthermore, there's the other trouble—the possibility that they might say no to the terms, and then, upon seeing the presentation, feel embarrassed about wanting to change their minds. So instead we hold back on the negotiations, and make the presentation upfront.

By this point we've researched and brainstormed the product enough to know it is patentable and profitable. We've got patent applications and written statements; we've got ideas on function and aesthetics. Hopefully in the time leading up to this point we've been holding onto everything that relates to the product—sketches, old parts, rough working models, computer renderings, etc., because we need to prove that the product works. We also need to show what it might look like; the viewers should not be trying to imagine for themselves the final result. We want to provide it from the very beginning, and to make it as easy as possible for them to get excited about what lies ahead.

We'll want to have both a brief single-page abstract of the product and a brief cursory outline of its benefits, as well as a rough working name for it (although considering the way that licensees seem to have a love for product-naming written into their marketing DNA, we try not to get too excited about anything that we think up). If it's in any way possible, we find that it's best to have a presentation ready before the first licensing meeting is even so much as scheduled. Sometimes opportunities might crop up very suddenly and it's necessary to pull something together at the last-minute, but it's really not ideal

In going into the meeting, we find it's best to keep in mind that the meeting's purpose is simply to establish whether or not our audience is interested: we're not going to cut a deal in one afternoon. There's a brief period of breaking the ice—introductions, small talk and so forth. I've usually got a jacket without a tie, and maybe that sums up the general tone: we don't want to seem like we're there for an interview, but we do want to be polished. In terms of demeanor, it goes without saying that we want to be as courteous and professional as possible and avoid speaking uncharitably about anybody else we've met with in the past.

As a rule, we make it our practice to offer up a sampling of our background before all else. It only makes sense to start off by establishing credibility, and so we begin with something of an inundation— a brief, quick-paced (and strategically overwhelming) montage of the hundreds of products on which we've worked. There are fitness products, there are medical products, there are children's toys and household supplies and anything else we ever have put out.

Once the background demonstration is through, we lay out a selection of products that we think could be suitable to them. Usually at some point before the meeting, we will have already spoken over the phone to get an idea about which of our products would be best to share. What they're interested in varies; they could be looking specifically for products that would be appropriate for short-form ads or products that would be appropriate for long-form,[16] some companies love fitness products, for

---

[16] See glossary for more on short- and long-form ads

example, while others have no interest in them at all. We try to streamline their choices, and to avoid anything that does not pertain to what they do.

At some point early on in our presentation, we have to prove our product works. This is crucial—often the potential licensees will be accompanied by various members of their engineering or manufacturing staff for assurance and council, and on several instances early on we made the mistake of showing them the glossy renderings of the finished product before we had the chance to show that the mechanics were feasible. The trouble was, if the staff members looked at the finished work and said that it would never work, and if we then had to do our demo to show that, well, yes... it could, and it, er... did... —then we'd just made them look foolish in front of their employers. We don't want to make life difficult for anyone, and we certainly don't want to create enemies going in. So we make sure to prove the product's abilities as soon as we can.

We can of course make a physical presentation using the actual product, which is something we've done hundreds of times in the past. Ever since the emergence of flashdrives and iPads, however, we've come to prefer going in with one- to three-minute videos, eliminating the need for us to haul around large models.[17] Going digital is also more convenient for the transference of information across geographical divide. We can arrange to get an NDA from our potential licensees, set up a time to Skype or conference call, guide them to our video site while we have them on the line, then, after giving them our login information, remain on standby as they watch the video. If they have any questions or misunderstandings, we are able to address them right away.

At the end of the presentation, there's a certain point where I essentially shut up. I just. Stop. Talking. If your meetings are anything like ours, you may experience the cringe-inducing silence that can permeate the room for full minutes of time once everything is done. Don't give in and try to fill it. Because there's almost always going to be a burning desire to apologize for the product, to start pointing out what could be better, simply for the sake of having something to say, and although that self-deprecation might seem very natural at the moment, silence is by far the better decision. Because when one of the team members finally does break the silence, it often is to say something along the lines of, "Well, I'm not sure which version to

---

[17] We'll usually bring a backup copy of the video in case of technological glitches.

choose—there are a handful of them that look good to me."
You would have killed that right away if you'd gone ahead
and started putting yourself down.

If and when our product does appeal to the
prospective licensees' sensibilities, we take the cue to
inform them that we will send them the deal summary. We
tend not to leave the product or the video with them after
this initial meeting; once we've gotten past the negotiation
and the executive summary, we may leave models with
them from time to time, but doing in the early stages is
generally unadvised. The question of premature exclusivity
might come up at this time, requesting that the product not
be shown to anyone else while the potential taker takes
time to think things over. Although it's great to hear that
kind of enthusiasm, the innovator cannot afford to comply
until serious negotiations have begun.[18]

If in the end the prospective licensees tell us that
they don't think the product for them, we don't push it. We
simply go on to the next product, if there is one. We might
say that we'll get ahold of them the next time we've got
something we think they might like, but the general idea is
to refrain from ever getting personal or persistent. Their

---

[18] In select cases, it may be agreed that prospective licensees have
exclusivity for a set period of time provided they pay a fee.

rejection might not even have anything to do with whether or not they liked the product. It could have been that the tooling was too high, or that they weren't experienced enough with that type of product; it could have been any number of things. But whatever the situation, we don't want to attempt to license to a company that feels hesitant about the product. We figure that if what we have really is good, we will eventually find somebody else to take it on.

David and Goliath
(Hint: you're not Goliath here.)

It's a bit of an endeavor, but essentially what I would like to attempt just now is to give you a comfortable sense of the relationship that goes into a safe and balanced licensing deal. You should know what is necessary to require of the people that you will be signing on with, and what is normal and reasonable in what they in turn require of you. To be able to sign your name without any cause for reserve or hesitation in your mind—it's the most solid and promising start that anyone could ask for.

If this is your first time approaching potential licensees, it's perfectly natural for you to find yourself carrying a certain degree of apprehension. You may feel like the proverbial fish out of water; you may be painfully conscious of the fact that you are coming to the meeting as a lone individual and not as a company, and it could be that you are sensing all the pressures and intimidations that stem from that fact. The firms' attitudes don't always do much towards calming these insecurities. Though there are many that will be gracious about seeing what you have to offer, others will make you feel as though you ought to genuflect before you sit down at the conference table.

But whatever impression they may give you, be it lofty or accommodating or anything that's in between, the truth is that they need designers. When an actual comparison is made of the number of individuals who market and sell things with the number of those who can develop a marketable, profitable product, it's clear that that the innovator is by far the scarcer commodity. It can be easy to lose sight of how much you have to offer. If you are one of those people whose mind is naturally wired for innovation and design, there may be moments early on in your career when you actually feel almost uncomfortable about accepting money for your work—it comes so naturally to you that you can actually question its value to others. You need to keep yourself in check with the realization that the specific artistic, mechanical, and innovative instincts that you're attuned to are in fact a complete mystery to many marketers, just as the skills of being a successful marketer are in turn a mystery to you. So. Know your worth. Remember that not everyone can do what you do.

You deserve to have the sense that when you sit down at the table with potential licensees, it is as equals— even if the company itself does not initially share that opinion in the least. Be professional, be reasonable, be honorable, but be ready to cordially leave the table if the fit just isn't right. It's like a marriage in a way—it kind of kills the spirit of the thing if you have to twist their arm into saying "I do." As such, I do everything in my presentation to bring up the good points of my product. I answer any questions. I clear up what misunderstandings there might be. But I don't try to talk them into it. If they don't feel strongly enough about it for them to be guaranteed to do a good job with it, then we ourselves will turn them down. It isn't that I mean to sound cocky, but there is no sense in licensing a product to a company that isn't going to do a good job with it. If this is something that is going to be done, it should be done correctly.

All taken together, the whole thing has got the potential to be a pretty frustrating little system at times, but believe me that it's a good system, and a necessary one. A manufacturer can't get far marketing something that's badly designed, however well-advertised it is. A designer's work, no matter how beautifully crafted, will simply sit in the shop if there are no marketers to put it out into the world. The symbiosis that exists between the two professions is what allows for there to be fine products on the shelves, and I suspect that's something accepted and respected by both parties in the end.

Before I speak any more deeply about negotiation, it should first be clear that there have been whole books written about the topic—scores of them. They were certainly not written by me. I'd like to have that right here on paper: that business is not my forte, it was not what I studied in school. But I've learned a lot through trial and error, and so whatever wisdom is to be gained by those successes and those failures, here it is at your disposal.

At Splane Design, we try to avoid getting too indignant over licensees demanding more than what is "fair." We know it's every businessman's obligation to cut the best deal that he can for his company. We know too that standards differ across the world, and that there are various cultures whose very norm is to press for more and more advantageous terms, however imbalanced they might be, until one finally is told "no." We can try to be understanding of this when it's something that we come across. But it gets to a point where if we are to have our bread and butter, we have to stand our ground. We're not in this as a hobby, and so certain measures of self-preservation must be taken.

The contracts that we propose are designed to be very even-handed, with no irregular clauses and no surprise departures from what our deal summaries first led the company to believe, and so the *average* business that we work with concedes that all is fair and fine. I suppose that what I mean to say is that none of the problematic issues I am about to address are what could be called "typical." Still, they have arisen from time to time. So. Without further ado.

One thing that's never up for negotiation is our stance on indemnity. If they insist that they are not responsible for covering us legally, we don't have to worry about anything else—we go home. Because once the manufacturers are in control of the product, they're completely in charge of what happens to it. They can cover the toy that we've just designed with razor blades if they feel like it—our hands are tied. Without being indemnified, our company runs the risk of being sued by an angry public for mind-boggling sums over product flaws for which we may honestly have had no part in. To our minds, our indemnity requirement is a perfectly logical way of going about things. The licensees don't always see it the same way. In truth, there are companies that have seen it so differently as to request that we instead indemnify them—these are multi, multi-million dollar firms—and when in our incredulous rejection of the idea we've wondered whether anyone has actually gone in for something like this, the response has been that it was their job to try to slip it in. Once that bit of fine print was identified and they were called out on it, they had no problem with taking it out. But they'd been good with giving it a go.

This is one trouble you may run into when working out a deal. A more probable problem, however, is the chance of coming across a company that is eager to reduce your percentage of royalties. When we first started licensing, the average royalty for a mass produced product was usually about 5%. After the emergence of the DR industry however, an attorney friend of mine shared with me some writings of his regarding why it was fair and allowable to accept lower royalties in the case of an infomercial agreement, and we thought his reasoning was just. As a result, what we came to accept as our new standard was a 3% of gross from infomercial deals and 5% from those with traditional marketing sources. Since then, we've had companies from both camps say they would like to bring that 3% and 5 down to a 2% and 4, perhaps lower still. While we understand that they feel obliged to negotiate to do this, we try to make them understand that the difference between 2 and 3% means a 50% difference for us, while for the licensee it doesn't even come to 1%. Invariably they will counter this argument with the observation that they've got extensive risks to be rewarded for, and that only a small number of the products they take on will be a financial hit. But the fact of the matter is that we ourselves scrap nine tenths of our own projects, and we would be thrilled if so much as 10% of what was left over ever made a good deal.

So we tell them: up until very recently, the universally accepted norm for designers' royalties was 5%. It took most of us a while, but after certain changes of circumstance we finally came to accept having to take less for our work. If however, we are now being asked to lower our 5%-for-traditional-firms and 3%-for-DR further still to

3% or 2, respectively, we might by extension soon find ourselves lowering to 2% or 1. What we are bringing to the table is more than a just sketch on a napkin. We are putting out multiple models, we've done refined design and engineering; sometimes we even do packaging and graphics. This is a long way from something rudimentary. So at some point we have to wonder—look, is 97% of the deal not good enough for you—do you really have to have 98?

On similar lines, we are somewhat tense when we come across firms that reject the formality of our being granted advanced royalties. On these occasions we explain to them, with apologies for any confusion, that our upfront advances are only advances that are paid back out of royalties, and are by no means a matter of greed—but that it is important almost to a point of superstition with us, and if they are still in a position to work with us after understanding that, then we hope they won't hesitate to call so we can carry forward with the deal.

To be perfectly unguardedly frank, the reason for all the importance placed on these advances is that they serve almost as a sort of test in gauging the sincerity of the potential licensee. If their monetary output is nil, we can assume their personal commitment to the product amounts to such as well. To illustrate a perfect example of this—I can remember visiting with a product scout who was telling me about how, in his interview for a position for a specific DR firm, the company brought sixteen different products to the conference table in order to show him what they had in stock. He was shocked—why, he wanted to know, did they even *need* him... just look at all these innovations they had on their hands. Their response to him was casual. We didn't pay anything for these licenses. We have the right to these products for a year, but we invested nothing when we signed. Maybe if we feel like it, we'll bring out one out of the sixteen. But really—these are easy come, easy go.

There's another reason behind our requiring advances from our licensees-to-be. Apart from needing some kind of collateral, we want to know that the companies we are about to put our faith in are indeed financially sound. On several occasions we have gone through deals with big established corporations only to find out that the whole time that we had been working with them they had been in the midst of some serious financial straits. In refusing to provide advances, firms will often run with the argument that they are going to be investing a good deal in our product through tooling and inventory and advertising and so forth. To this I can only reply that if

$25,000 is that sizable a sum in their business's eyes, then it's difficult not to question the issue of whether they truly have the funding to do the thing at all. The truth is, we have received bonuses as high as $200,000 in our line of work just for signing on the line. What we are requesting of them is by no means extreme.

It's easy to read the situation as a done deal against you; with advances in particular the initial refusal seems to come out more as resolve than as reluctance, and there's a definite sense of finality when the infomercial company flatly states that they do not provide upfronts. Take heart a little, and try to hold tight. It's been our experience that once we've shown these companies the actual product and they've had a moment to get excited about it, exceptions get made.

Lack of guaranteed exclusivity is another roadblock with certain firms. Everyone wants the comfort of knowing they've got the corner on marketing the product all throughout the world, and we're happy to give that to them. But it cannot be just for safekeeping. If they are only really going to market in the United States, why are we going to give them the whole of Latin America? As far as we're concerned, they can have exclusivity everyplace where they can establish, or have established, significant marketing ability. That is the caveat in the material—that they have to have a true licensing presence for what we're giving them. Half our income comes from international sales. If they make a hit in the U.S. and don't have any serious plans for taking it international, we have no problem with licensing to someone else.

Something of a distant cousin to the issue of international exclusivity is that of marketing companies wanting to reverse royalties on international sales. It's not unheard of for them to come back after the agreement and to try to make a case for giving us a lower rate on foreign royalties, claiming that the business of marketing overseas presents all sorts of heightened expenses that we need to be sensitive to. This is nonsense. By the time that they've done the show in the U.S. and are moving on to foreign sales, they've already paid for tooling, packaging design, trademarks, script writing, video production costs—a huge amount of work has been prearranged by virtue of it having been done first when marketing to the States. And so if we were going to go about deciding how much of a royalty we get based on how much an additional expense cost they're experiencing, then what they pay us for international sales should actually be higher than what it is.

From time to time we come up against some disagreements over patent funding. The status quo for our company is that we regularly take out provisional patents, but rarely do we take out the patents themselves. By our contracts, those patents must be applied for by the licensee in the licensor's name and at the licensee's funding, and the patent rights must revert to the licensor once the license no longer is in force. To someone unfamiliar with patent processes this might seem demanding, but in the industry it's very much routine. In fact, most licensees tend to prefer to have us stay out of the way where patenting is concerned. For one thing, they don't want us to burn time on the life of a patent. If we were to license a twenty-year patent on our own, it might still be five years before the product got signed onto by any licensees, and that means five less years for them to profit by it. Furthermore, there is the matter of our being a relatively small company. We don't have anywhere near the necessary funds to patent a product in every corner of the world—which is what we would have to do if we filed for our patents personally, since after a domestic patent is filed, the owner of that patent (along with anybody else) has only a short amount of time before he loses the right to file for further patents outside of the States. All things taken together, there's a perfectly logical case for why we conduct things the way we do.

Every now and again, however, we wind up with a licensee whose terms stipulate that we come up with fifty percent of the patent fees. In these instances there's not much to do but to bluntly explain that A) if they're anything like most people we work with, they actually really don't want us to be the ones filing the patents, and B) that with them signed up to be getting 95% of the profits, it isn't particularly logical or pleasant for us to be paying 50% of the cost. Most often once it's presented to them in this new light they very courteously give it up. I might put out a 5% compromise just to smooth things over if they push the issue, but to be truthful, if a licensee is nickel-and-diming us as early on as this, we usually start reconsidering just what it is we're getting ourselves into and whether it will be worthwhile.

If we get past the deal summary and they tell us that we're close to an understanding, then we're all right to move forward with the contract. We work quickly in getting this done. As silly as it sounds, it's easiest if we fill in the blanks and send off our agreement as soon as everything's a go, so that we will be able to use our own template as a starting point rather than having to read through theirs to see what amendments we'll need to make. Sometimes they'll insist on using their own, and so sometimes we'll combine them. But the fact to be conscious of is that we are licensing the product to them, not the other way around, and it only makes sense for the contract to be offered by those who are, in fact… doing the offering.

Specificity is essential where matters of agreement are concerned. I would love it if it were possible to simply have all business settled with a handshake, but even among friends there can be completely honest misunderstandings regarding what is being agreed upon. I can remember one particular company that attempted to get things done by sending out an agreement that was only one page long— this isn't the way to go. A licensing agreement has to be written out with particular care; it's a time when you really want an attorney stepping in for you and doing your work.

Something worth remarking upon is that the deal that I write is never "padded" for negotiation. It seems to be a common assumption among some groups that initial demands are intended simply as a starting point, that when someone names their terms they've taken into account all the whittling-down and hard-bargaining that it's going to undergo. Maybe I'm not being very clever about this, and maybe you'll find it's best to do things differently, but I'm a firm believer in the notion that it's best to speak in earnest from the start. It's simply the way I do things—this is the deal I'm asking for, nothing more and nothing less, and if it's close to what they're willing to go for that's great, but if not… why even bother with the song and dance?

One point of routine caution regarding contracts: over the years, we've found it's best that we do not sign the agreements before we send them out. If the prospective licensees end up tweaking the document our names are signed on and then print it out and sign it themselves, then we could be unwittingly agreeing to all manner of stipulations we have never seen. Because of this I tend to send the document as a PDF file, with the hopes that it will be somewhat more difficult to alter, and if they do send it back signed I make sure to have someone lay the different versions over one another on top of light tables to ascertain what we're signing matches right with what we sent. It all sounds very cloak-and-dagger and Perry Mason and whatnot, but every now and then we're given good reason to have caution of this kind.

In going through this whole process it is important to understand that these firms are very often are in possession of their own legal departments whose role is to whittle you down, and those legal departments very often are moving in a very different sphere from the managers and the guys in sales and marketing whose goal is to have the deal go through. Communication between the company's departments is not always what it should be; there have been times when a CEO has phoned us up to check on how the project's going, only to find out that we've been struggling with their legal department trying to get to where we can begin our work. And sometimes we never do begin it—when the negotiations just go on, and on, and on, you get to the point where you have to simply contact the president of the company and say you need to move on. At moments like this, there is nothing we can do other than explain that it'd be great to maybe do another deal with them sometime in the future, but that we've been grappling with their legal department for ages and just can't get this this thing to go.

One last thing we haven't talked about is the idea of licensees occasionally looking to put a cap on your earnings, saying for instance that they'll pay you three percent until you've made a million dollars, at which point they don't owe you any more. The way we see it, there is no reason why the innovator should not be making a profit for as long a time as the manufacturer is. Unless they're donating everything to charity, there isn't any good reason for cutting us off. Now, if they have to freshen up the product in order to extend or renew their patent, we do agree to work with them at no cost. But the product is theirs only on lease. We haven't sold it away. So the bottom line is that we don't go in for caps on IP. It's probably not something you're likely to run into; we don't have it asked of us very often anymore. I *have* had it happen though—so if it does occur for you, just know that that is how we manage it.

Much of the time, the CEOs of the firms we work with will work to give us the impression that we're in this endeavor together as partners. And we are, to a point. Everyone's more or less on the same side here, wanting the same good outcome, and in the spirit of good fellowship we'll try to be sympathetic to their point of view in whatever reasonable ways we can. But when it gets to the point where we're being pressured to back them up in impractical ways, putting their profit above our responsibilities towards our own small firm, then we try to make it clear to them that we are an expense like any other that they have. Whether their business is doing well or poorly, their landlord gets the same steady sum from them on his monthly rent check. Their insurance company isn't going easy on them in their tougher times; their mechanics aren't giving them a break[19]. We'll try to act as a partner in many ways... but don't be fooled. We are the "rent" on the intellectual property.

　　If all of this is simply too overwhelming to manage on your own, you may find it worthwhile to take on another party for negotiating assistance. This is not at all an irregular road to take. Even with the company we met with just today— we were not negotiating with the president of the firm himself, and I was not there personally to negotiate with the fellow that he sent. As long as whoever's standing in for me knows me well enough to gauge my judgment, it's a fairly effective system that allows me to put more time and concentration into doing what I do best. It also tends to put the two companies just another step further away from getting into any kind of an inflamed situation. You certainly don't ever want to get to the point where you're in danger of raising voices or slamming phones; that goes without saying. Both of you must let yourselves have whatever distance and detachment and time that it may take to get your wits about you.

---

[19] Pun inadvertent—but feel free to appreciate with due distaste/mirth.

It can get a little itchy, this business of working with companies who make it their duty and routine to test your limits. But what makes matters even more complicated is knowing that there are also going to be companies that will be beautifully compliant with all of your terms, but whom you would be better off turning down. The reasons for having to do so vary. It could be that you sense they don't have the expertise needed in selling to your specific market; it could be that they lack the business smarts. Or it could be for no perceptible conflict at all. There's nothing trivial or dismissible about a gut instinct, and if we get an uncomfortable sense about the individuals managing a firm—or if we begin to hear of moments when they've been less than truthful in their dealings in the past— we consider it a perfectly legitimate motive for stepping back and moving on.

But know that there are honest firms, too; don't ever let yourself go forgetting that. There are firms you will trust, and trust with good reason, and under whom your products may enjoy years of safe handling. I don't have any lengthy passages addressing them here—by the very nature of their decency, there isn't that much to relay—but they're there, and that knowledge is a source consolation and a cause for true respect. You cannot guarantee that you will always be surrounded by these kinds of even-handed firms, but by the manner in which your own firm chooses to conduct its business, you can ensure that such firms at continue to at least exist.

Somewhere in all this, as we've said before, the only real power you have is to bow out. That will always be there for you. In any event however, it should ease your mind to be aware that difficulties of negotiation are to be anticipated in any business setting that there is. May they be truthful, may they be gentlemanly— and God help us, may they be brief.

Contracts

By now we've spent an awful lot of time going over how to manage problems that the licensing contract might present. However, we haven't taken much time to discuss the original contract itself, regardless of how disastrously or successfully it might be received.

Now, a quick (if redundant) disclaimer: I am not equipped to give out official legal advice, and I wouldn't want for that to be forgotten. I will give my interpretations of what a viable licensing agreement includes, but know that you cannot rely on me alone. When you embark on all of this you must have lawyers at your side.

Typically, the contract begins with "Warrantees and Covenants," saying that both parties have the right to enter into an agreement. From there we go to "Non-Competition," granting the exclusive rights to the product (if we in fact have given them exclusive rights, which is often but not always the case). It's here that the licensee[20] agrees not to let anyone else manufacture or market the product at hand. Then it's necessary to describe the product, to establish what it is that's being licensed via a description, patent, or provisional patent number.

The next clause addresses any additional products, informing the licensee that any permutation of the original item would be subject to royalties paid to the designer. In other words, you've got to make sure they aren't able to change a couple of buttons and then not owe you anything out of the proceeds. This same clause can also extend to state that you as licensor have got a right to be included in a share of whatever profits may come from any related accessories and sell-through products, whether or not you

---

[20] Brief refresher (because it *is* confusing): licensee= them, licensor=you

designed them yourself. Essentially, you are requiring that you be paid for any derivation of your work.

The license goes on to declare that the licensee is in charge of funding the manufacturer, the tooling, the inventory, and the shipping costs as well. Our contract also has a section where the licensees agree to provide us twice a year with samples of what is being manufactured, and to return what prototypes we lend them within sixty days in near-original condition so that we don't lose time repeatedly building new versions.

Our legal indemnity as licensors is addressed over the course of the agreement as well, for the same reasons that were mentioned before. Even though we will give the licensees our advice and drawings and samples and so forth, they are the ones that have the final say on what they come out with. Sometimes the final decisions that they make are so questionable that we are ashamed to even be associated with the product, and so we actually make a point of saying in the contract that we can take our name off of the product if we choose. But when it comes right down to it, we don't *want* to be a part of the final say. If we had the rights to make alterations and control quality, we'd be mixed in with the blame for any unwise choices that the company might be sued for, and our basis for our indemnity would be shot.

Next comes "Insurance." The licensees have the responsibility to pay for and maintain liability insurance, and are required to send us certification of it before they make their earliest sales. It's important, because if members of the public are somehow injured, the licensees, if uninsured, might be forced into such desperate measures as attempting to sue the licensor in order to fund their defense.

"Television Production" gets covered if we are working with infomercial companies; the document lays out whether it's to be long form or short form or a "spot," and establishes that the licensees are going to be responsible for the production and the cost. The contract must also cover legal compliance (the licensees are the sole guardians of the thing's legality) and "Test Marketing Rollouts" (i.e. putting down a date and milestone for when they will send us proof that they have shot and test marketed the product). The writing goes on to state that if the test market is successful, they'll commence with the rollout as promptly as is possible, and if it is unsuccessful, they need to notify us that about their plans to terminate the deal. Furthermore, they promise to promote, sell, and distribute at their own expense and to make all the reasonable efforts towards a success (holding the responsibilities for shipping, credit cards, and so forth).

As far as the "Rights to Intellectual Property" go, you should know that you generally want to license the rights, not assign them, and that you should not automatically sign papers that assume you're assigning. When you license you are giving the right to manufacture and to market the product, but you are not giving away the product itself. When you assign, everything is theirs. Sometimes there's a tax advantage to assigning, since the money that you get from your royalties will be classified as long-term capital gains. But if something should go wrong for the product or for the company, an assignment could lead to some difficulty in your regaining your property. Because of this, we tend to keep to licensing, and if we do assign, we write up the agreement so that the assignments are very much like licenses in the sense that the product is technically owned by the licensees but reverts to us in the case of their going bankrupt or defaulting.[21]

---

[21] There *is* something to be said for the use of assignments if you are purely interested in a single upfront lump sum, no royalties involved. In fact, as we ourselves explore non-licensing options (self-manufacturing, e-commerce, etc.) we are looking more and more into assigning away product rights. But this is a matter of handing over the product rights, being paid for them outright, and forgoing all future

We've talked before about what reverse engineering is; there are again precautions made against it here. By our contract, it is understood that the licensees are not to try to change the product in order to get around having to pay our royalty, nor are they to allow this to be done by any third party with whom they have a deal. The work is ours, the patent is ours, and unless for some reason we've assigned instead of licensed out that patent, we are going to be paid for any version of the product that comes out.

Next, the "Exclusive Right to Market" section outlines the various marketing methods that might be used, be they television, print, radio, retail, e-commerce, catalog, or home shopping networks; it covers whether or not the company will be marketing worldwide, and illustrates how broad or narrow a market they are permitted to address. (For example, you might grant the rights to sell to consumers at large but not the rights to sell to hospitals, since you might have another version in store that is for hospital use only.) This same section also makes note of the fact that we don't allow the licensees to sublicense without getting our leave, and that none of their rights go into effect without our receiving the agreed upon advance

---

involvement in the product. There is a difference between that and selling the rights when what you mean to do is license them.

within ten days. In some cases we might lower the amount, but it is important that the sum is paid.

Also in the contract there is some talk of "Minimums." For each twelve months, they must send us a minimum royalty, the amount of which changes depending on what the product is. I've got a friend whose father licensed a product with no minimum royalty, then realized that the company's reason for taking on the product was that it had been potential competition for a product they already had. They had nothing to lose by pretending to want to produce his product and then keeping it shut away indefinitely, and that's exactly what they did.

This section is typically followed by a portion of text discussing "Compensation." As stated before, we feel that on any licensed product there ought to be some form of a down-payment, which we the licensors may agree to pay back out of our first royalty (assuming that that first royalty occurs) and without which the license does not go into effect. This is also usually the moment when the "Rollout Advance" gets addressed. In that first moment when the TV ads start airing and the call centers are set up—when everything really is happening and the product is for sale— then there's often an advance that's offered from the licensee to the licensor. These rollout advances are different from the signing advances previously mentioned, and they are peculiar to the DR world. The thing is this. If they pay you a rollout advance and the product turns out to be unsuccessful, they have lost a good deal of money. If it is successful, you pay the advance back out of the royalties anyway. In essence, they end up putting themselves into risk over a situation where no one really wins in the end even if the best of circumstances should transpire. So, knowing this, we'll often have a section in our contract informing them that they don't have to worry about rollout advances (or if we do decide to leave it in the contract, we'll often reduce it from what it originally was). The fact is, these licensees are making plenty of concessions to us; it's good to be able to lighten their own burden where we can.

Now, "Royalties." We won't go out of our area of expertise by putting out exact percentages in terms of how high or low a royalty an innovator should require. The appropriate number varies so much from case to case, depending on whether you're working with limited or high volume (the higher the volume, the lower the royalty), whether it's high-tech or low-tech (higher technology yields higher royalty rates), and a whole slew of other factors. Whatever the percentage is however, it should probably be based on gross sales, meaning that the percentage that you are granted is one that is based on the total income minus shipping-and-handling and any money paid back to the customer upon a product's return.[22] There are people who offer a much higher percentage—maybe even half— at net sales, basing the percentage on the dollar amount of a sale after costs are deducted. It sounds like the better deal, but we decline these and stick to gross, because net sales would mean that they could be writing off everything—coffee breaks, lunch with clients, lunch with crew... and to manage this, you would have to stipulate everything that they can or cannot write off, which would get fairly fussy and tedious. Furthermore, for the sake of transparency the licensees involved in a net deal would have to send the licensors the bookkeeping of everything that is being written off, which amounts to a load of documentation every time they send a check. The truth is, I personally just don't want to bother with it. So we keep to gross sales.[23]

You've got to cover "Accounting" to some degree, more or less just to state that they need to send you clear (though not necessarily extensive) royalty accounts. We

---

[22]"Net sales" is sometimes used to mean this, but this is a misnomer.
[23]The exception is if they are offering free product, where there is nothing paid but shipping and handling.

also use this section as an opportunity to set forth how payments are to be made. Our standard and preferred method is to have a wire transfer done straight to the bank so that we sidestep the confusion of the check being in the mail, but there is still always the option of payments being sent in the form of a check. The crucial thing is that we choose one way and stick with it, so that it's easy to keep track of what transactions have been made. Also, it's important to establish just *when* the royalties are due. We like to keep it on a month-to-month basis because the more frequently the check is sent the more systematic and habitual it is for them to have it in on time, but many companies would rather send it in by the quarter and we've got no big argument with that. There's some forgiveness for lateness built into the contract regarding all of this. The license might stipulate that the check is due within, say, ten days of the end of each month, or within a month of the end of the quarter. But it must be paid relatively on schedule.

The section that deals with "Terms of Termination" tackles how long the agreement's good for; it also talks about how the licensor may terminate the agreement if need be, or how the licensee in turn may end it, if that should be the case. Sometimes there is a termination fee when the licensee decides that things might end, but by that point it's usually too difficult to extract it from them for it to be worth writing into the deal. There are different types of termination, but the most substantial and relevant one for our purposes here is probably the one known as Termination for Material Breach, meaning that the contract is being finished off due to the fact that one side or another has failed to uphold what was agreed to in the contract. Most often there is a period of time beforehand for them to make amends, and that's often accounted for in the text, but if worse comes to worst, termination is indeed a choice.[24]

Within this section the sell-off period must also be addressed. Once the contract is terminated the licensees are not allowed to produce any more units of the product, but that isn't to say that they aren't given any time to sell however many are left over from before the deal was killed. This period of selling off what's still on their hands is called their sell-off period, and they owe the licensor royalties on whatever they do sell in this amount of time even though the contract's done.

[24]Force Majeure usually is found poking around somewhere in these regions of the text. We won't go too far into it, but basically it's this. If there's some kind of natural disaster— an earthquake, a tidal wave, anything along those lines—we usually allow for some time before everything reconvenes. For the sake of reality and everybody's better good however, that recovery period can't simply be endless. So if they're not back on deck within a specified amount of time, we end the contract.

Finally, the section wraps up with the establishment of "rights and duties upon termination," essentially stating that if and when the contract's over, the licensees lose the right to manufacture and sell the licensor's product, while in turn the licensors may lose rights to any commercials or logos or artwork and so forth.

Because the whole process does so often become bogged down in terms of timing and efficiency, we have what we call Continuation Fees. If a company we have licensed to has been too slow with a product, then instead of having them automatically lose the license we have it written into the agreement that they can opt to buy more time before the contract reverts to us through the payment of a pre-agreed set of funds. Now to be perfectly frank, if we know that someone really is working hard at hitting their milestones and they happen to have hit some genuine setbacks along the way, we probably won't enforce the continuation fees. But it's good to know they're there in the contract, so that we do have that option in the moments where we have cause to believe we really are being led down the garden path. The licensees can sometimes get to feeling a little indignant being charged for not being on time, but in all honesty, the fact that we allow them to pay these fees at all is something done in their own interest.

We're giving them a safety net; it's their second chance to save the contract. If they don't want it, then they can very easily not pay it, and terminate the deal. But we'd rather not have them have to go through losing a product in which we know they have invested quite some time. Frankly, we'd rather not begin all over again with different clients either, if it can be helped.

So there you have it. There are other templates you can find online; these are just the bare bones of our own. We've redesigned the full document a couple dozen times over throughout its lifetime to make it as acceptable as could be for both licensor and licensee; it's a living document, something that's intended to be subject to amendment and to change. But I'd venture to assert that it's proved itself fairly strongly in the years we've had it at our side.

A Final Word About Licensing

I don't think that we are alone in wanting to start stepping back from work with infomercial companies; I think there are a number of other innovation firms that have quietly begun to do the same thing. I hope that these individual efforts to preserve the dignity of the creative industry will improve the terms that creatives are being offered. But until then, we recommend that if you move forward with licensing, you do it with caution. There's a good deal to be gained in it, but a good deal also at stake.

—

A Designer's Abbreviated Look at Marketing[25]

Generally speaking, the designer of a product is not expected to be the one to go out and promote it; that's what marketing companies hire advertisers for, and if something goes wrong and isn't on the up-and-up where all fairness and disclosure is concerned, it's usually the marketing company that it hits. With that said, no one involved in the overall process can count themselves invulnerable when it comes to legalities, and so for the sake of having at least a sketchy understanding of what is or is not legal, here are some general parameters that might be good to know.

Earlier we spoke about the concept of continuity marketing—about a system where you just keep sending them the product in a slow and steady stream, either because it needs refilling or because the product is of a serial nature where there are always new additions to be had. This is also known as "advance consent marketing," and although it can be a blessing, there are also some failings involved. Primarily they are to do with the fact that the people who are enrolled to pay these regular

[25] Acknowledgements— Planit, Michael. *Operators are Standing By*. N.p.: Mc Graw-Hill Companies, 2007. Print.

installments often don't realize that they're making them at all. This is frequently the fault of the marketer, who all too often is quick to encourage the buyer into agreeing to fine print that he or she has not had the opportunity to grasp the full significance of. Even if it weren't for the fact that a lot of cracking down has taken place over the past several years, a wise seller would do well to keep things "above-board."

The whole concept of fine print in general is a particularly delicate matter in advertisement regulation; any precautionary advice or clarifications of potential misconceptions must be placed in clear view, according to the rules set forth by the Federal Trade Commission (for reasons obvious to anyone with an ounce of justice in their veins). The monitoring of this stipulation became trickier than usual with the advent of the internet, at which point a scroll bar and a million unique web-page layouts suddenly muddied the question of what was or was not a suitably obvious and visible place for a disclaimer to go. But although it's still difficult to put the management of this sort of thing into sturdy concrete terms, strict tabs are still kept on online marketing, and by no means is it to be looked at as an easy vehicle for consumer deception.

In spite of a certain degree of twenty-first century skepticism over things that seem "too good to be true," free offers actually tend to be pretty popular among the American public, and can often be a productive way of boosting a product's visibility and regard. However, whatever is being offered up as free must really truly be so if it is to escape being cracked down upon by the FTC, and anything involved that demands payment requires full warning and disclosure on the advertiser's part.

However small the ever-catchy word may be, "new" is never taken lightly in the advertising world. There are clearly defined rules regarding at what point in its existence a product is or is not permitted to be "new," with six months standing as the usual amount of time between debut and expiration. Tricks like trivial changes in a trademark don't justify the claim that something's newer than it is, and to try to stretch the truth is dangerous because even if the FTC doesn't catch something, a competing company could be keeping an eye out for false claims that might be used to bring their competition to court. Also, it's wrong.

Testimonials in advertising can be helpful. They bring in a personal element and boost the credibility of the design. But if the givers of the testimonies deliver a message that is disproportionately enthusiastic, or if the speakers have perhaps yielded unusually positive results, the advertiser must to go beyond simply adding a flimsy "results not typical" onto to the ad. Great lengths must be gone through to ensure that it's obvious that it really, no really, is not as great as your user is making it seem. Come to think of it, in the end you might actually be better off just gagging the guy and having him frog-marched out of the studio ASAP.

When celebrities are the ones giving the testimonials, we enter into a whole new realm of complications. A great deal of emphasis is put to the idea that their personal commitment to the product must be genuine, i.e. if a celebrity says he or she uses a product, by law it has to be because they actually use it, and so forth. (I highly doubt they've actually got a troop of attorneys that march into Natalie Portman's bedroom every morning to certify that she sprayed on her Dior, but the idea still is that you keep things on the level more or less.)

One sound piece of solid advice: the marketer, and if at all possible you yourself as the innovator, should make certain to be present at video shooting in order to keep tabs on everything that's going on. But for the most part, as long as everybody keeps their noses clean and their heads on straight and doesn't seek out more than what can be gotten honestly, there's not much to be afraid of where marketing's concerned.

E-Commerce

There are simpler ways of marketing intellectual property (IP) than the heretofore traditional approaches. The emergence of e-commerce has opened a huge vista of possibilities for companies like ours. After so many years of having to have leagues of sales reps out beating the pavement, we're honestly a little smitten with this whole idea of not having to knock on Wal-Mart's door—of making the full ten dollars from a ten dollar product rather than a percentage that translates into maybe fifty or even thirty cents. Furthermore, the beautiful irony of e-commerce is that it's got the capacity of actually completing the circuit all the way back to infomercials in the end. What often happens is that if a product is successful in e-commerce, the infomercial companies may request the rights to sell it—and very often will make a better offer than they would have originally.

There is EBay, Amazon, Etsy, and Alibaba (often touted as a "Chinese Amazon."). There is also crowdfunding. For those who aren't familiar with this twenty-first century phenomenon, it started with two separate websites called Indiegogo and Kickstarter around

2008 and 2009, and has been growing exponentially ever since. Essentially, someone with something new presents their product to the greater crowd on cyberspace, stating how much has to be raised in order to fund it and explaining the different rates at which people could choose to invest, at which point the public (for the sake of personally owning the product as well as for an altruistic desire to see it succeed) puts money behind it. Usually there are reciprocal gifts involved or samplings of the new product, but it is at heart a greater-good system—a sort of Wikipedia of innovation-funding, so to speak. Crowdfunding doesn't apply well for design companies like ours that are systematically coming out with new products—we'd have to be asking for help from our family and friends again and again—but for an individual with a single stand-alone product it can be a great tool.

More recently we turned our attention to www.quirky.com, then still in operation and relatively new, with an online community of roughly 900,000 members and a growth rate of about 2,000 a day.

The premise to Quirky was simple. Anyone, without payment, could submit an idea online. Once received, the submissions were categorized (i.e. kitchen, exercise, etc.) and displayed on the website for public feedback. Like the crowdfunding sites, Quirky would ask its users to vote on the products. However, unlike crowdfunding, they weren't after investments; the votes existed simply to gauge the product's appeal and potential.

Then, every Thursday evening at seven p.m. Eastern Time, Quirky would hold an online-televised reviewing process for the most highly-rated ideas. After presenting each idea to a live studio audience, Quirky's panel would conduct an open discussion on the product's merits and drawbacks. Ultimately, the discussion would end with a show-of-hands vote, while members from around the world typed in their own comments in real time.

Both the in-person votes and the online opinions were factored into the final decision of whether or not the product should be produced and marketed under Quirky's name. Although the public opinion was valued, however, it was not permitted to seize control. The Quirky staff reserved the right to review its products internally, and if the head innovators saw merit in a particular product, they could elect to accept it for development even if it lacked a strong following. It was a novel approach, and one that was important for a couple of reasons. For one, it stopped the voting process from turning into any kind of a popularity contest. For another, it also got away from any petty school-aged tactics of I'll-vote-for-you-if-you-vote-for-me. But most importantly, it helped Quirky retain its credibility. It made sure that the best products were the ones that got released.

If all went well, Quirky accepted the idea, which they then designed, engineered, prototyped, tooled, manufactured, and marketed. Contribution to this process of refinement could come from any Quirky follower who could lend their skills, sources, or ideas. They might come up with an engineering solution or conceptualize a design aesthetic; they might help choose a name or even just a color. It was collaboration in the grandest sense. In the end, Quirky either marketed the product themselves or rolled it out to big companies to be sold in everyday stores.

Quirky worked by assignment, not by license. When they took on a product, they actually owned it; it wasn't theirs on loan. However, they still payed the innovator royalties as if it *were* on loan/license—6% of gross sales went to the innovators and 4% to anyone else in the online community who aided in the product's development. This was the best of both worlds for the innovator; it provided profits without responsibility. And Quirky was good about being noninvasive: throughout the early stages of development the innovator was given ample opportunity to take the idea back, with the stipulation that if Quirky happened to have already started work on it, they (Quirky) would simply receive 10% of any royalties that resulted from the licensor one day licensing the idea to someone else. And so it made for a fairly even-handed exchange.

For all its assets, however, Quirky was still a relatively young system, and it was still in the process of fine-tuning some of its operational details. In our own experimentation with submissions, we ran into a few things that we sensed had the potential be problematic.

Some of them were policy issues, such as the fact that Quirky was not required to take out patents, and instead primarily relied on the advantage of being first to market. It was a gamble that failed to take into account the fact that should anything go wrong, the innovator could no longer legally patent the idea once the product was made public.

Other drawbacks were matters of practice. Quirky had a tendency to over-alter many of the ideas it accepted, as well as to rely excessively on computer renderings in lieu of physical models. Additionally, their brainstorms ran very brief, and there were certain voting issues, such as allowing children to cast ballots, that seemed less than ideal.

I contacted Quirky to mention these points; I was very much pulling for their success, and it seemed logical that I might be able to make myself useful to them by sharing what I'd learned as a product designer. When we did meet, however, I found that they themselves had already identified the very same conflicts that had stood out to me, and had been searching at length for equitable ways to resolve them. They were interested in brainstorming, and we corresponded on the topic for some time, but in the end we were equally at a loss. There were simply no easy solutions to the issues at hand.

Quirky ultimately filed for bankruptcy in September of 2015. I'm not informed about the exact reasons and conditions for its having closed its doors, but it was evident that they were facing certain unavoidable impediments that would have been difficult for any company.

As discouraging as it was to witness the end to such a promising startup, I believe it's a sign of great progress that websites like this are taking form in the first place. In spite of the necessary fine-tuning that will have to be done on any similar sites that follow, it's my belief that the concept could succeed, and that if it does, it will be outstandingly beneficial for the world of design.

—

DreamProjX, the Master's Course:
Designing a Life

If you go back to the beginning, our aims were always simple ones. Even when we got ourselves into trouble with the big office, my goal wasn't trying to be the man wearing the heaviest cufflinks or writing with the most expensive pen; there was never any Gatsby wonder-quest. I wanted the comfort of having a modest home where my wonderful wife and I could raise a couple of children, and I wanted this to be earned by taking hold of the opportunities that happened through working hard at what I loved. It's always seemed to me that when all is said and done, the lucky ones among us are those that are able to laugh and smile the longest and most often in the years that they are given.

When I was working in the big office I wasn't doing much of either, and I knew I had to make amendments to my way of work—and so, being a designer, I designed my new life the way designers are trained to design anything they do. I went through all the automatic motions, knowing that design does not begin by simply picking up and sketching, it begins with words and analogies and models for what one is trying to create. I charted up factors and parameters until they looked like something off a police inspector's blotter; I made lists and bullet points and color-coded arrows that zigzagged through the page. Really, it was a matter of compartmentalizing, of taking a sketchbook and mapping out the different elements of my life—personal, physical, financial—and seeing how these individual columns might meet up to make one goal. The DreamProjX model in all its fullness was meant to be more than just a model for just making money; it was a model for realizing one's dreams, and this may be the most important thing we have to share.

Now, you can call it balance, or fulfillment; I know there are a lot of terms that everyone from psychologists to yoga teachers use. For me, though, it was always the word "confidence" that got jotted on the page. Because that was as close as I could get to describing the thing that I was striving towards: confidence, steadiness, whatever was the opposite of fear. Fear causes fatigue, and fatigue so often turns fast into illness, and if you have fear, fatigue, and illness—it's devastating. You see the effects asleep on cardboard in the streets.

Financial confidence is a tricky one, in a way, because our culture's relationship with money is so conflicted in and of itself. We are taught that competition's good, that the American Dream is not only our birthright but our moral duty to pursue. And yet it's not that simple. Wealth is both glorified and sneered at in the world we live in; we drive past newly-slicked billboards that stare us down with the alluring reminder that diamonds are a girl's best friend, then we turn our attention to the radio and hear "Daddy Never Was the Cadillac Kind."

It differs from family to family. Some teach that it's good to be proud of one's successes and of the drive that is behind them. In the family I grew up in, however, describing a person as particularly ambitious or enterprising was always a euphemistic sort of shorthand for saying that they lived by a different way of thought. And that passes down. I've got a daughter who gets antsy just being in a sports car with the top down. She's a Splane, and it shows in her thinking—that second-nature fear that people might start thinking that you're showing off.

I don't know that I would change that. But there's a kind of inconvenience and restrictiveness about this way of looking at things. They say aim for the moon and even if you miss it, you'll land among the stars. Well, if the stars are all you mean to ask for, where should you be aiming? Because I'd hate to point my metaphorical arrow at what is simple and sufficient and have it send me sailing straight down to the surface of the earth.

Furthermore, there are advantages to wealth that aren't of a glamorous nature. I'd like to approach old age without having to worry for those relatives who are approaching it alongside me. I don't want to be without means when a family member is ill and needs to see a specialist. I'd like to not be powerless when I witness a hard-working person fall into a spiral of difficulty that a simple loan of funds could fix. It'd be a terrible thing— to look on at any of these situations and to realize that the one reason I was helpless was because in my mind making money had been something ugly that was linked with buying a big watch. So I do aim for financial confidence, because in spite of the fact that I'll never really lose my old Splane thinking, I've come to recognize that we are no longer hunter-gatherers, and that while money can't buy happiness it can buy some safety for the people whose existence *is* my happiness and in fact my peace of mind.

So then. We allow ourselves to do our best in making money, and try not to be ashamed. Personal confidence, now:

What makes up personal confidence is going to be a very different outline for every individual. To me, confidence in my person is impossible to have without a sense that I am doing well in carrying on the integrity and consideration I was raised to carry; it's something very much to do with not wondering what I would do if asked to stand my ground on what was just and right. It's a matter of knowing that I'll be dependable for those who are in my family and those who might as well be; it's being true to my word and to my obligations, and understanding myself to be a man who isn't only trusted but who has earned that trust.

I think that whatever certainty of character I have comes from the moments when I decide to be straightforward about what I am, and what I know, and what I want, as well as what I am not, and do not know, and do not want. It comes from a sense of self-reliance in being able to look at situations that I'm expected to view as challenges and to instead grip onto them and work them into something manageable and maybe even advantageous in what I want to do. It's like back when I was a climber. It was deadly to think there might be a thousand feet of empty space below you and a terrible overhang above. All you could do was concentrate on the piece of rock that you were on right at that moment. Or it's like when I was teaching martial arts: when you go to break the board, you don't punch it thinking, well, here's to my chances. You go to break the board. And it's become a corny line, this whole thing of "you either do it or you don't," but the message isn't compromised just because it has been used in too many action films and slogans—it is as true now as it was in all the centuries before it ever came to be cliché.

This personal confidence as it relates to my own life is also a matter of my being able to plan for the future while I live for the moment, and to simply be my utmost through it all. In my toughest years of education and of working, whenever I would get perplexed by something daunting that I knew would be approaching, I'd find myself returning to the knowledge that the best I could do was *all* that I could do, and that it was the only thing anybody had a right to ask of me. Only if I know I haven't worked my hardest do I have cause for shame. As I get older, part of this has come to mean just being the finest version of my age that I can find it in myself to be, and maybe that's where "physical confidence" comes in. At this point of life I certainly wish I had the health and the physique of someone in their twenties, or even in their forties, come to that. But all that I can do is all that I can do. If I didn't allow for that, day to day living would be a very frustrating thing.

But enough said about that. Going back to the idea of this exercise, this whole concept of being able to design your life…

I think we all get our certain share of opportunities in life. Admittedly, we all know some poor bastards who just can't catch a break, these guys who've got little gray clouds following a foot above their heads while they walk around getting pinged off cliffs by giant swinging hammers. For the most part, however, the prospect of never having lucky opportunities is actually unlikely. The only issue is that if we haven't got a picture of what it is that we want to be doing, we aren't going to be prepared to recognize our share of these advantageous happenings in the moments when they happen by. So it isn't only positive thought that turns things around. It's organized thought, it's clarity of thought, it's seeing in specifics. Essentially, that is what this exercise is. It's taking a personal inventory of one's skills and one's desires and seeing where they overlap—seeing which obvious but heretofore unnoticed course of action might present itself when one gives it the chance.

I half want to say you can put anything you like onto your lists, that there are no boundaries at all. And yet there *are* certain rules, if this exercise is something that you're going to do. One is that you must be honest—not only in regards to those things that you're bad at, but about your strengths and talents too. For some reason, there's only one thing in our culture that people feel they can admit to being good at, and that is cooking. Well, screw the spaghetti. You can't be modest when you do this: if you do, the process just won't work. Now, the strengths I'm talking about don't have to be limited to specific hobbies or skill sets; it doesn't have to be that you can pound out a concerto or split the center arrow on a target clean in two. I look at my best points *not* in terms of which machine I'm most adept at or what type of drafting programs I know how to use—when I think about my assets what comes to mind are things like the fact that I can operate as a generalist, or that I can function as a one-man band. Your own points might be that you are good with people. Or, instead, that you are someone who could work alone without just going insane. As for the weaknesses— truthfulness does not necessitate negativity. I could say that I hate stingy people, or I could say that I really enjoy generous ones. They both mean the same thing. But it's a little like driving; if you look at the object you don't want to hit, you end up smashing into it.

The other rule is that you have to go into as much detail as you can. Once my own lists had given me perspective on the changes that I had to make, Miriam and I made some lists between ourselves in regards to our hopes for our new life. And we gave ourselves permission to just go crazy with it. We turned ourselves loose. Did we want to live near the coast or near a river? In the mountains or below? We accounted for things like having an airport within sixty miles, having cultural centers somewhere nearby, being down the road from hardware stores and welding shops and yards of lumber or of scrap.... We took it down to the most meticulous of descriptions, then traveled to our would-be home locations where we tried the whole thing out like children playing house. The long and the short of it is: you don't go about your planning by filtering out the ridiculous or the small, at least not at the onset. No; if we're going to do this, let's go all the way. What kind of flowers do you want growing on the studio porch? What color are you going to paint the door? Maybe it doesn't sound very three-piece-suit to be talking about all these little bits of silliness; maybe even in the privacy of your own notebook you feel some inhibition about using anything but solemn generalizations regarding your "direction" and your "field." But when you've got a true excitement about something that you really want to do, you find your mind starts painting that front door. It starts imagining the very sound of the doorbell. And the more fully you envision just what it is you wish that you were living, the more fully you're fulfilled when it all comes to be.

If someone were to look through those old lists of mine today and then look at where I am and what's around me, it would seem as though the lists were not a plan but an after-the-fact description of the dream. We came just that close in finding what we'd set out to find. Certainly, there were some small compromises and departures from our vision when we encountered it in person; the house was still unfinished and in the rural regions San Diego County rather than the rural regions of the Central Coast. But construction would be finished soon, and the newfound location carried all the beauty of the original ideal—plus members from both sides of the family within an hour away. It was sixty minutes from a city, but had clean air and had space; it was a short drive to the seaside, but from our windows we still could see the mountains where in the wintertime it snowed. There were steel yards and real hardware stores that I'd have easy access to, and dirt roads where the kids would later catch rides in the backs of neighbor kids' pickup trucks. The orchards were beautiful, the earth was fertile and the terrain was flat enough to use. What wasn't there we'd build. And that just kind of solved it. From then on, it was all a matter of the doing.

I've had so many of my best imaginings come true that it almost is unfair, and when I realize how close to the top of the global pyramid I live, the idea of being open to more seems almost like a kind of sin. But! I shrug and I try for the new dreams anyway. And one of the nicest things about realizing these ways of finding happiness is that I get to hand them off to other people to use for themselves. Because whatever kind of successes I have had or confidences I've been able to develop, it's still like it used to be back in my old backpacking days: it's the experienced packers that have to be sure to help the new ones along.

I've been so lucky in the journey. I'd have thought that by this age I'd be coasting, that I'd have my foot-rest and my wingback chair and an unexcited understanding of where I'd be five years from now.

It's nothing like that at all.

—

We hope you enjoyed reading about our search for creative freedom and economic independence. If you are interested in spreading the word to friends or colleagues who might share our goals, they can be referred to our website, www.dreamprojx.com, to our Facebook and Twitter accounts—keyword: Splane Design.

Glossary

Note: Definitions appearing below are skewed to the context of this book.

Designer: Ideally, a creative individual who blends art and science to inflict their notion of the perfect arrangement of form, line, proportion and graphics on an un-expecting public. Can often be seen running about with colored markers and open scissors.

Innovator: Any designer, inventor, engineer, artist, scientist, entrepreneur or person who creates anything unique.

Design methodology: A roughly prescribed, but efficient, means for solving problems and generating innovations or designs.

Brainstorming: A semi-organized exercise in generating innovative ideas. Often performed in small wildly gesturing groups

Provisional patent: A low cost program made through the U.S. Patent Office, by which any person can send in minimal documentation and a small fee to give their invention "patent pending" status for twelve months

Design patent: A patent based upon the decorative elements of a product or design

Utility patent: A patent whose claim are based upon the function of an invention

Foreign patent: Patents filed in foreign countries

PCT: (Paris Convention Treaty) Signed in 1882, the PCT provides for international filing of patents. Among the benefits of the treaty is that it can be used to "hold your place in line" enabling a designer or inventor to pay a fee and postpone for a time the greater cost and effort of actually filing of a patent in individual foreign countries.

I.P. (Intellectual Property): Patents, copyrights, trademarks, trade secrets, programs, processes and any other rights to the innovations of man kinds mind.

Licensing: The granting of certain rights to an intellectual property (usually the rights to the marketing and sale of an I.P, and often the right to manufacture).

License: The agreement, contract (or license) document used in granting rights to something of value.

Assignment: Differs from a license in that, rather than giving licensee prescribe rights to a product, it actually transfers ownership of the intellectual property (I.P.)

Licensor: The owner of a product, process, or other "object of value" who licenses specified rights to another person(s), company or organization

Licensee: The person, company or entity receiving the licensed rights

Gross profits: The full dollar amount received for the sale of a product or service etc. (usually minus shipping and returns)

Net profits- The dollar amount of a sale after costs are deducted.

DR (Direct Response): Infomercial

Infomercial: DR (Direct response)

Short-form: A television show or commercial that is usually just under three minutes long

Long-form: A television show or commercial that is usually just under thirty minutes long

Indemnity: The granting of freedom from prosecution or law suit.

Product liability insurance: Insurance offered to protect (primarily) inventors, owners, licensees, manufacturers and marketers of products or intellectual property, from negative economic exposure, usually as the result of law-suits for products which are claimed to be dangerous, deficient or ineffectual.

Corporate designers: Designers who are employed as in-house designers for a specific corporation or company.

Consulting designers: Designers, either independent or in a group, who are hired by outside firms or individuals to perform design-for-hire on their behalf.

Design manufacturers: Designers who manufacture their own designs.

Design educators: Design professionals who teach design-related skills.

Orientation brainstorm: Usually a brainstorming session that occurs early on in a new project. Includes both orientation to the project and preliminary idea generation.

Design brainstorm: Brainstorming sessions that concentrate on aesthetics or styling.

Angels: Investors, often friends or family, who make a loan, a gift, or an investment towards a particular venture or idea.

Crowd-funding: A new means of raising capital where the innovator makes a video pitch of their idea on specific internet sites, often offering some kind of premium in exchange for contributions to the funding of their goal.

Investment breakfast clubs: Breakfast meetings that are organized to introduce prospective investors to inventors or entrepreneurs.

Nondisclosure agreement: Also called an "NDA"— an agreement to keep a secret from being shared, often in regards to a new design, invention, process or business plan.

Continuity sales: Usually involves automatically scheduled sales of a product or service. A good example would be acne creams where refills are automatically sent to the customer monthly and the transaction is charged against their credit card.

Reverse engineering: Redesigning a product or other innovation to avoid patent infringement or royalty payments.

Continuation fees: Fees that may be paid in order to extend a licensing agreement's expiration date.

Deal summary: A brief summary outlining the major terms of an agreement.

Self-manufacturing: In the traditional sense, the term represents an innovator/entrepreneur who manufactures their own designs, doing the major portions of the work in their own facilities. It can also be used, however, to describe the process in which an innovator/entrepreneur manufactures their own innovation(s) by sub-contracting out the actual manufacture or work.

Processes and Materials

Processes:

Shape/sculpt

Cut & piece

Car case

Weld

Braze (furnace)

Dip braze

Solder

Friction weld

Sonic weld

EMA weld

Heat stake

Hot plate weld

Solvent weld

Bond

Fasten

Snap

Wedge/ interfere/ clinch/

Swedge

Thread

Telescope

Wrapped

Woven

Sewn

Knitted

Heat sealed

RF sealed

4 slide bending

Tube, rod & strap
bending

Bent laminate

Stack laminate

Composite laminate

Machine

Turned

Screw machine

Rolled

Cold drawn

CNC (machined)

Mill (CNC)

Ground

Shape

Profiled

Panagraphed

Saw/cut

EDM/wire cut

Plasma cut

Water cut

Sand blasted

Photochemical machined

Photo engraved

Laser Cut

Stereo Lithography

(Other Rapid

Prototyping) LOM, Fused

Plastic (Stratasis Co.)

Injection Molded

- Plain
  Injection
  Molded

- Co-Molded

- Low-Pressure
  Injection
  Molded (Bo
  Jackson,
  Hettinga)

- Cole Injection
  Molded
  (Catalyzed
  Mtrls.)

Injection/Compression

Gas Injection &(Liquid

Gas Injection see

Hettinga)

Mold Insert (& In Mold

Decorating)

Metal Injection Molding

(MIM)

Ceramic Injection

Molding (CIM)

Transfer

RTV

Compression Molding

Blow

Roto Molding

RIM

Dip Molding

Wet Pressed (Ceramic)

Dry Press (Ceramic)

Vacuum Form

Pressure Form

Twin Sheet Pressure

Forming (w/ foam in ctr.)

Slump Form/ Blown

Strip Heated

Die Cut

Scored/ Perf Cut

Hand Blown

Electro Plated

Sprayed

Cast

Sand & Ovo Process

Sand Casting (Vacuum)

Die (Plaster Mold,

Graphite/Gravity Mold,

Die (ZA8, ZA12, ZA27,

Mg)

Die Cast W/ Co-Molded

Plastic or Rubber Skin

Investment

Powder Metallurgy

Catalyzed Resin

Slip

Lay Up

Hand (W/Gel Coat)

Chopper Gun (W/Gel

Coat)

Transfer

Vacuum Bag

Extrude/Pull-trude

Co-Extrude

Wet Extrude (Ceramic)

Form

Break

Roll

Stamp

Nibbled

Punch

Blanking (& Fine

Blanking)

Coining

Concussion

Deep Drawn

Hand Drawn

English Forming Wheel

Die Formed

Spinning

Hand Thrown (Ceramic)

Compression Formed

(Ceramic)

Pressed

Forged/Wrought

Finishing/ Decorating:

Emboss

Engrave

Etch

Laser Mark/Engrave

Bonderize

Peen

Bead Blast

Tumble

Brushed

Polish

Plate (Chrome, Black
Chrome, Ti-Ni, Brass,
Cad, Gold...)

Case Harden

Hard Polished Stainless

Vapor Polishing of
Plastics

Vacuum Metallize

Galvanize (Zinc
Plated/Hot Dipped)

Japan Black

Oxidize

Bluing (Or Browning)

Patinas (Viridian)

Anodize/Hard Anodizing

Iridite (Any Metals,
Many Colors)

Bleach

Wax

Oil

Stain

Spray Paint
(Lacquer/Epoxy/Enamel)

Powder Coat

Baked Enamel

Pad Print

Screen Print

Flexography

Hot Stamp

Gold Leaf

Color Wipe

Decals

Substrate

Formable Dry Painting
(In Mold Painting)

Hydrographics (Floated Inks or Decals on Water & Transferred On)

Off Set Printing

Flocking

Materials:

Gases

Liquid

Plasma/Energy/Light/Magnetism

Stone

Graphite

Crystals, Gems

Chemicals

Plaster

Concrete

Ceramic/Clay (& Synthetics)/Porcelain

Enamels

Silica

Glass

Bone, Tooth, Shell

Leather (& Simulated)

Hair & Bristles (& Simulated)

Carpet

Fabric

Molded Fabrics (Fabrics W/ Foam… Nylon, Wool, Polyester, Cotton)

Plant Fibers

Synthetic Fiber

Rope

Webbing

Cork

Sponge

Paper/Cardboard/Corrugate

Pulp/Papier Mache

Bamboo & Rattan

Woods:

Soft

Hard (Exotics)

Man Made

- Molded

MDF

Plys

Masonite

Masonite (Molded)

Petroleum, Tar, Amber

Waxes

Plastics:

Thermal

ABS

P.E.

P.E.T.G.

Peek

Macroblend (Polycarb. &

PETG Polyester Alloy

From Mobay)

P.P.

PVC

Polycarbonate

Acrylic

Acetate

Styrene

Butyrate

Vinyl

Ultem

Noryl

GE Fortran PPF (30%

Glass filled, Good to

Over 500 Deg. F)

Thermal Sets

Epoxy

Bakelite

Delrin (Delrin= common

commercial name; a.k.a.

"acetal")

Nylon

Teflon

Sheet Metals

Plastic Laminates

Board Materials

Corrugated

Shapes (Rode, Tube, Bar,

Rod, Etc…)

Heat Shrink

Recyclable

Glass Filled

Composites

Re-enforced

Fiberglass

Kevlar Fibers/ Carbon
Fiber/ Graphite Fiber/
Ceramic Fiber

Foams:

Soft

Fabrifoam (Fabric and
Foam)

Rigid

Styrene

Urethane

Vinyl

PVC

Open Cell/Closed Cell

Self-skinning

Insulating

RIM

Elastomers:

Rubber

Neoprene

Crayton

Nitrile

Santoprene

TPR (Thermal plastic
rubber—injection
moldable)

Silicone

Vinyl

Urethane

Metals:

Ferrous

Iron

Low Carbon Steels

High Carbon Steels

Spring

Stainless (300 Series, 400
Series)

Chrome Moly

Non-Ferrous

Copper

Beryllium Copper

Brass

Zinc (Zinc/Alum. Alloys
ZA8, ZA12, ZA27, G.M.
Patented Alloys)

Pot Metal

Tin

Lead

Aluminum

Titanium

Magnesium

Gold

Silver

Exotics & Alloys

Forms:

Billets

Rod & Bar

Tubular

Foils

Sheet & Plate

Pre-Finished

Laminates

Alucobond

Extrusions

Screen/Hdwr. Cloth

Expanded

Embossed

Corrugated

Pierced

Cable & Chain

Design Elements:

Line

Contour

Form

Volume

Weight

Scale

Balance/Angle/Unbalance

d

Positive & Negative

Space

Tension

Structure

Geometric, Organic,

Amorphous, Ergo, Fluid

Symmetry, Asymmetry

Flexibility, Rigidity

Motion, Kinetics,

Dynamism, Fluidity

Function

Finish

Depth—Transparent,

Translucent, Opaque

Reflectivity

Illumination

Value

Color/Hue

Texture

Pattern

Graphic Composition

Materials Choice

Mood

Associations

Secondary Uses

Recyclable

www.ingramcontent.com/pod-product-compliance
Lightning Source LLC
Chambersburg PA
CBHW050441290526
45786CB00006B/2112